ROBERT OH

LIVING *Like*
Kierkegaard: 2023

Contact Email: oikosbishop@mac.com
Dr. Bob Oh YouTube: https://tinyurl.com/5knavyrw

I dedicate this book to

Pastor Samuel Choe

Who taught me and so many of us
how to follow
the leading of the Holy Spirit God
in demonstration -
To take our cross daily
And Follow
Our Lord Jesus Christ.

"To me to live is Christ"
Phil. 1:21a

4

Table of Contents

Introduction

Let the year of 'Black Rabbit' begin!

According to Jong Ang Daily the following was stated: Where does this annual phenomenon come from? Koreans, along with many other Asian countries, tend to categorize the years based on the lunar calendar, using a 12-year zodiac cycle with 12 animals — the rat, ox, tiger, rabbit, dragon, snake, horse, sheep, monkey, rooster, dog and pig — cycling around to represent each year. In 2023, it is the Year of the Rabbit.

Koreans call the lunar animal years ddi, which roughly translates to sign, and are used when referring to the year in which they were born. There are also set beliefs that people have distinct tendencies, and even fortunes, shaped around their *ddi*.

This is why you may have witnessed your daily horoscope told based on what year you were born in and what animal you are associated with in Korean newspapers, magazines or portal sites.

Although the trend of people categorizing and identifying themselves has now largely been taken over by the Myers-Briggs Type Indicator (MBTI) personality assessment, *ddi* has been around in Korea far longer, with mounting piles of interesting phenomenon and anecdotes accumulated over its history.

Specifically, though, 2023 is the year of the black rabbit. Although the Year of the Rabbit comes around every 12 years, the black rabbit year comes in every 60 years, meaning the last Year of the Black Rabbit was in 1963.

This second layer of categorization is derived from five elements also incorporated in the Chinese zodiac: water, metal, wood, earth and fire. The zodiac animals move through the different elements, each associated with a color, each time they complete one 12-year cycle. Essentially, there are 12 animals and five elements, making for 60 years of different combinations.

The year 2023 is the year that the rabbit matches up with the water element, which is associated with the color black in the Chinese system. Hence, it is the year of the black rabbit.

I dedicated 2023 as the Year of Refusing to Do Nothing Daily! The result of doing something daily that matters eternally can be seen in numbers below. PTL!

2023 by Numbers:
- Sermon: x852 times. 71 times per month on the average.
- Books Published: x21
- YouTube: 53,700 views, 3,200 hours, 449 New subscribers (Total: 1,107)
- Academia.edu: 17,979 Pages Read, 724 Down loads.
- Countries Visited: x6 – USA, Cambodia, Korea, UK, Denmark, Thailand.
- Flight: x37

I want to 'live' like Søren Kierkegaard. I met too many people wanting to talk about existential philosophy but refusing to live as an existentialist! Most likely, Søren Kierkegaard would not want to be identified as an existentialist, but he did start a philosophical movement called 'existentialism.' Maybe we can just try to copy and try to live like Søren Kierkegaard as just a Kierkegaardian!

I composed a poem, pearling Søren Kierkegaard's thoughts in one place. What I did in this year 2023 can be represented by so many of the points from this poem – becoming that individual!

Who is a poet?
He is an unhappy man who conceals profound anguish in his heart. Yet whose lips are so formed that as sighs and cries pass over them... they sound like beautiful music.

"Love does not alter the beloved", he says,
"it alters you."

Love is all, it gives all, and it takes all.
So, don't forget to love yourself.
Don't become indifferent.
Don't become a stranger...
At the bottom of enmity between strangers lies indifference.

Be free!
Be that self which one truly is.
You will lose control, do not fear anxiety...
Anxiety is the dizziness of freedom.

During the first period of a man's life,
the greatest danger is not to take the risk.
Not to be anxious...
Not to be free...

You are free, indeed. Yet...
How absurd you are!
You never use the liberties you have, and...
You demand those you do not have.
You have freedom of thought, but...
You demand freedom of speech,
freedom from finance,
freedom from social injustice.

Ah, because you who as a physical being always
turned toward the outside,

thinking that your happiness lies outside,
you finally turn inward and discover that
the source is within you.
Face the facts of being who you are inside...
for that is what will change who you are outside.

Jump! Have faith in God...
If I am capable of grasping God objectively,
I do not believe,
but precisely...
because I cannot do this...
I must believe.
I must jump!

The paradox is really the pathos of intellectual life
and just as only great souls are exposed to passions...
it is only the great thinker who is exposed to what I call
paradoxes, which are nothing else than grandiose thoughts in
embryo.

It is in this imperfection of everything
You can attain your desire -
by passing through the opposites.

Take away paradox from the thinker...
and you have a professor.

So, Jump! Have faith in yourself...
Become that self which one truly is.
It is so hard to believe because it is so hard to... obey.
Faith is the highest passion you will ever experience.

Faith is a snare,
you cannot have it, without being caught.
You cannot have faith in such a way that you catch it,
but only in such a way that it catches you.

So, Jump! And live your life to the fullest...

10

Life can only be understood backwards;
but it must be lived forwards.

Life's hidden forces can only be discovered by living.
The highest and most beautiful things in life...
are not to be heard about,
nor read about,
nor seen,
but to be lived.

Purity of heart is to will one thing...
To be that Individual..
Desire it. Think it. Meditate it...
Our life always expresses the result of our dominant thoughts.
You are ripe when you have made this truth your own.

Also, be careful about what you dream.
Old age realizes the dreams of youth:
look at Dean Swift;
in his youth he built an asylum for the insane,
in his old age he was himself an inmate.

Jump!
And pray your life to the fullest...
Pray like you have absolutely nothing to do.
Why are you so busy?
Who are you busy for?
You pursue pleasure with such breathless haste...
that you hurry pass it.

It seems essential, in all tasks, that you concentrate..
only on what is most significant and important.
Far from idleness being the root of all evil,
it is rather the only true good.

Pray like you are in love.
Just as in earthly life lovers long for the moment,
when they are able to breathe forth their love for each other,

to let their souls blend in a soft whisper,
so long for the moment,
when in prayer you can, as it were,
breathe forth your love to God.

Prayer does not change God,
but it changes you who pray.
It is God who will fashion you..
God creates out of nothing.
Wonderful you say.
Yes, to be sure, but he does what is still more wonderful:
He makes saints out of sinners.

If you do not jump, you will be bored!
Boredom is the root of all evil - the despairing refusal to be
oneself.

I begin with the principle that all men are bores.
Surely no one will prove himself so great a bore...
as to contradict me in this.
Since boredom advances and boredom is the root of
all evil, no wonder, then, that the world goes
backwards, that evil spreads.

This can be traced back to the very beginning of the world. The
gods were bored; therefore they created human beings.

Gods created them to JUMP! -
The only way out from this boredom.

How do you become that Individual?

Do not let the world give you a name...
If that is not you.
Once they label you - they negate you.

Don't be afraid to become that Individual!
There is nothing with which every man is so afraid

12

as getting to know how enormously much he is capable of doing and becoming that Individual.

Don't expect world to understand you.
The world understand me so poorly that they don't even understand my complaint about them not understanding me.

Don't fight with the world.
Quarrel with the world is completely fruitless,
whereas the quarrel with oneself is occasionally fruitful...
and always, I have to admit, interesting.

To dare is to lose one's footing momentarily.
Not to dare is to lose oneself.

So, I dare you...
to become that Individual.

Jump!

January

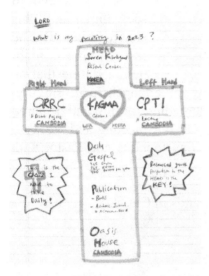

I received this diagram on Nov. 30, 2022. Out of 7 small 3M stickies I wrote independently came this cross. The head of my 2023 cross is continuing work in Korea for the Soren Kierkegaard Research Center. Heart of the cross is my work at KAGMA. My right-hand work is my research in Cambodia through CRRC. My left-hand work is at CPTI. The Daily Gospel is the center of work doing 730 postings per year (365 in Korean and the same in English). Out of this work, books are published and posted at the Academia.edu site. Finally, my grounded work is through Oasis House as I set this ministry to become self-sustainable as we retire from Cambodia.

1/1: Catalyst Church Sunday - Preaching on Jan. 1st.

Pastor Barry has Covid-19 and asked me to share a message on the first Sunday of the year. I am amazed at his humility and openness for a guest speaker to open up the year for his people. The amazing thing is that on the first Sunday of last year, 2022, he had Covid-19 as well. I declared 2023 to be the year of refusing to do nothing - daily!

1/2-3: Orange Canaan Church Revival Meetings
Pastor Kim Inchul texted me as asked me to lead two days revival meeting for his church beginning of the year. He shared that I gave

him my poetry book 20 years ago and he was blessed by my poems.

Well, there is a first in everything in life! I was so excited to see him and his congregation. But he texted me night before stating that he is in Emergency Room getting ready for an open heart surgery. What?! We spent time as one body interceding for him and declared a fasting chain prayer. God showed up at our meeting and we were blessed by His presence and His anointing together and Pastor Kim Inchul is recuperating fast – PTL!

1/6: A very special meal with a new friends in Christ.

There are people you meet for a reason, a season then for life! I believe I met a brother who's going to run the race together for long long time in Jesus Name!

1/6: Ministering at Jesus Church Small group gathering.
Jenny and I had wonderful time ministering at this intercessory group – all women group! Food was fantastic, and we basically shared out-of-life experience as they had so many questions about

16

how to live as a Christian counselor, intercessors and etc. They made a commitment to pray for our ministry as I share our monthly Love Letter with them.

1/7-9: Las Vegas Full Gospel Church.
I visit Las Vegas annually to hold a revival meeting at Las Vegas Full Gospel Church.
Pastor Joshua Kang launched $13 million dollar building project.

Robert Oh
Just now

Finished ministering at Las Vegas Full Gospel Church! I can not share what I did here, because what happens in Las Vegas stays at Las Vegas - so I was told! 😄

They sold the old building and has to move out by March this year. Oh Lord!! Only God can make that happen! So we spent lots of time interceding for that project to become a reality. Spoke 3 times in one Sunday as usual. Twice in Korean service and once in English service.

1/11: The miracle testimony of this month… maybe this year!
My friend Charley was diagnosed 4th stage blood cancer! We declared 21 days fasting – food & media prayer. Below is what I received from him.

Hi pastor Bob,

Thank you so much for your prayer! Good news: Doctor told me that my cancer is in complete remission! Praise God!!! All cancer cells are dead!!! THANK YOU for your prayer. God heard it and is gracious to me.

Wow! Cancer is completely gone! All cancer cells are dead! Thank you Jesus for saving my friend Charley! Our God is Johovah Rapha – One who heals!

1/12: Book Talk #123 on 'Finding my destiny' by Pastor Koh Sungjoon.

I started my 'let's read one book per week' campaign in Cambodia years ago, but not too many wanted to join – So, I just started posting regardless of anyone participating or now. Well, today I posted book #123! PTL! It's been so helpful for me to push myself to read a book per week and actually post it via YouTube on my Dr. Bob Oh TV.

Dr Bob Oh TV
▶ YouTube

BOOK TALK:
Finding my destiny
Author: Koh Sungjoon

As they say, "Not all readers are leaders, but all leaders are readers!"

I pray that more missionaries from Cambodia will join me in this personal campaign, and read a book per week to improve themselves and thereby better equipped missionaries in Jesus Name. Amen!

1/12: Lunch with Grace Mission International English Ministry pastors.

They say that as you get old, you have to do '3 Ups' – Show Up, Shut Up and Pay Up!

Well, these awesome men of God wanted to have lunch with me so I showed up, but they won't let me pay for the meal and asked many questions about life in ministry so I couldn't shut up! But they loved it and they want to meet more and asked me to lead a revival meeting in May – PTL! I am so happy my favourite wife wasn't there. I can hear her say, "Hon, you talk too much as you get older!" ☺

1/13: We met 30 years ago on our English Ministry Korean

American pastors' trip to Korea. He has been ministering in my city for ten years, but I did not know until last week. The associate pastor of Orange Cannan Church informed me of this information - PTL! What sweet fellowship we had in Jesus' Name!

Pastor Pang is finishing off his Doctor of Ministry thesis right now and I offered my service as his academic consultant!

I see many years of fellowship and ministering together – Thank you Jesus!

1/14: Mother's 85th birthday with the family.
My mother-in-law celebrated her 85th birthday with her family. It's a beautiful occasion, but also it's sad to see our mother getting old. Each year it seems she is becoming fragile and visibly weak. We blessed her for good health in Jesus Name. Amen!

1/15: New Life Oasis Church Sunday – Preaching 4 times in one Sunday. That's Korean style!

Title: The Year of Refusing to do nothing daily!
Text: Ephesians 2:10
For we are his (1) workmanship, created in Christ Jesus unto good works, which God hath before (2) ordained that we should walk in them.

International Standard Version:
For we are God's masterpiece, created in the Messiah Jesus to perform good actions that God prepared long ago to be our way of life.

Weymouth New Testament:
For we are God's own handiwork, created in Christ Jesus for good works which He has pre-destined us to practise.

(1) Workmanship (KJV), Masterpiece (International Standard Version), Handiwork (Weymouth New Testament): ποίημα (poiēma); Noun - Nominative Neuter Singular. Strong's Greek 4161: A thing made, a work, workmanship. From poieo; a product, i.e. Fabric.

Pt: I like International Standard Version – 'We are God's masterpiece!' The word used here 'workmanship (poiēma)' is used only one more time by Apostle Paul in Romans 1:20, "For the invisible things of him from the creation of the world are clearly seen, being understood by the things that are made (poiēma), even his eternal power and Godhead; so that they are without excuse." Apostle Paul applies this word to the 'works' of God in creation.

Pt: In the Old Testament, prophet Isaiah refers to God's creation as His handiwork.
• Isaiah 19:25 The LORD of Hosts will bless them, saying, "Blessed be Egypt My people, Assyria My handiwork, and Israel My inheritance."

Pt: But the next clause shows that Apostle Paul refers to the 'new creation' in Christ Jesus, as he continues in Ephesians 2:15, "to create in Himself . . . one new man." Apostle Paul makes the point that both we are simply God's creatures in 2Corinthians 5:17, "Therefore if any man be in Christ, he is a new creature: old things are passed away; behold, all things are become new" and in Galatians 6:15, "For in Christ Jesus neither circumcision availeth any thing, nor uncircumcision, but a new creature."

Pt: Apostle Paul is stating that we are created as a new creature through Jesus Christ to do good works, which is inseparable characteristic of those who encountered Him, as he states in Galatians 5:13, 14, "For, brethren, ye have been called unto liberty; only use not liberty for an occasion to the flesh, but by love serve one another. For all the law is fulfilled in one word, even in this; Thou shalt love thy neighbour as thyself."

1/16: Standing Stone leadership dinner.

What a wonderful fellowship and fantastic Korean food! Jenny and I are part of the Standing Stone ministry – Shepherding the Shepherds in America! About 1000 pastors quit ministry in America per month. These awesome retired pastors have been ministering to younger pastors by providing free counseling and mentoring to encourage and heal them. Jenny and I are so happy to be part of these leaders' lives. We learn so much from them each time we meet – PTL!

1/19-23: New York New Vision Church Revival meetings with Jenny

Jenny and I were invited to minister to this church last year. For some reason we couldn't fit the schedule last year, but finally we are here in New York New Vision Covenant Church – PTL.

Enjoying our first Utopia Bagel - the world's best bagel according to New Yorkers! Actually, it was very very good. Bit of their story on the web: Utopia Bagels was founded in 1981 in Whitestone, New York. Using the old world process of individually hand-rolling our bagels, kettle boiling them and baking them in our 1947 carousel oven with love by our experts. This process is what gives our bagels their distinctive taste generation after generation. We take pride in our bagels and know you will be able to taste the passion. See you at Utopia. Yes, Jenny and I can

22

testify that it was very good bagel. Sister Moon got us one dozen of them to freeze and take them home to our children.

1/21: Lunch with Suemee Hur of New Jersey. We met about 10 years ago in Cambodia. She came as a part of a short term mission team of New Vision Covenant Church.

Suemee posted following on her Facebook wall:
So grateful for these two vessels in the body, what a legacy they  have built and continue to build along with many of our missionaries that not only create for their own families but for generations of others. All of the spiritual children you guys have sowed into and have bore fruit and there is more to come! We only got to spend a few hours together but that was all I needed to be touched by all that they carry and all that they impart as people of His great healing love. Oh the stories, the testimonies that ONLY God can do, the God math, the miracles, signs, and wonder!

As we sat and broke bread together and they shared stories, testimonies of God's immense goodness. I was once again swept off my feet over His goodness and awe-inspiring, all-knowing Father that loves us so deeply. They have traveled the world for decades bringing hope, inner healing, physical healing, a Father's love, and so much more for His glory. I was reminded today in our conversation of the tension that many of us live in daily, but it's our journey as we continue to be refined, to walk in the process as we grow and are stretched, that things are easy with Jesus EVEN when we face the hard things. The reminder that truly, truly all that we live out is to be embraced as part of the story that will become a part of the journey.

And we know that in all things God works for the good of those who love him, who have been called according to his purpose. Romans 8:28

Thank you Pastor Oh and Pastor Jenny for being you, for all of the sacrifices that you continue to make to heed the call. Thank you for being a fragrance of His love and really being examples of the power and authority that fills a room because of how low you go the higher He brings you. We haven't seen the best yet, may 2023 be filled with the incredible things of God that no eye has seen. May it be for all of our pastors, our teachers, our leaders, our marketplace entrepreneurs, the body in 2023 to see the more of God in the most miraculous ways.

1/21: Soup Dumpling dinner to celebrate our 39th anniversary.

Look at Jenny's face! She LOVES it!! Little bit of history on the Soup Dumpling: While its origins are often debated, most agree that the xiao long bao's story begins in the Shanghai suburb of Nanxiang over nearly 150 years ago. It is believed that Huang Mingxian wanted to create a dumpling that would surprise and delight the guests of his restaurant, Ri Hua Xuan. Despite being created in China, it was the Taiwanese restaurant chain Din Tai Fung that popularised these palatable bite-size gems, and today, it has become a must-order dish during a dim sum feast.

According to Rubaa Shunmuganathan of Expatgo.com, this is how you need to eat Xiao Long Bao, the Soup Dumplings:

1. Prepare the sauce

Add a dash of soy sauce and vinegar in a small saucer along with

 finely sliced strips of ginger. For the best concoction, mix one part soy sauce to three parts vinegar. The perfect blend of salty and tangy liquids ensures the dipping sauce will complement the meaty pork filling well.

2. Dip carefully

Using your chopsticks, gently pick up the dim sum and lightly touch it in the dipping sauce. The thin dim sum wrappers are extremely delicate, so it's best to handle them with care.

3. Prick the wrapper

Next, place the *xiao long bao* on your spoon and slowly prick the skin so the piping hot broth oozes out of the skin. You can do this by either biting a small hole on the side of the dim sum or carefully poking the skin using your chopsticks. This step is vital, so do not skip it! Pricking the wrapper releases the steam inside the dumpling and cools down the broth so it doesn't burn your tongue when you bite into it.

4. Slurp the broth

Now comes the best part. Slowly slurp the scrumptious broth from the dim sum. This well-seasoned liquid will definitely get your palate ready for the next big meaty bite.

5. Enjoy the whole morsel

After sipping all the soupy goodness, gobble the whole dim sum down on one bite. Repeat steps 2 to 5 ad infinitum… or until you're properly satisfied.

Actually for Jenny and I, we dig in and eat as much as we can! I had these soup dumplings at Shanghi as well, but it seems New York Soup Dumpling are even better! ☺

1/23: Small Batch dining again.

We found a great restaurant at Long Island, New York. Jenny loved her experience at the Small Batch restaurant so much that she requested that we go there again – after her inner healing session with Pastor Martin, right before going to the airport! She is such a foodie. Yes, I eat to live and she lives to eat!

We loved their Cioppino last time with Suemee so we ordered it again at the Small Batch. Cioppino with Montauk striped bass, shrimp, squid, mussels, clams & grilled sourdough - $46.

I researched and found this history of Cioppino:

As with so many delicious Italian foods, Cioppino has an interesting history that developed from making the most of what you had on hand.

As one story explains, the genesis of the fish stew came from Italian immigrants who lived and fished off the San Francisco coast in the late 1800s. If a fisherman didn't catch anything that day, he would take a pot around to other fishermen, who would toss in any seafood they could spare. The mixture of fish, clams, mussels, shrimp, etc. would become the stew for the night. The tasty staple eventually become popular in Italian restaurants around the San Francisco area and then spread across the country from there.

Today, Cioppino is generally made from cooking seafood in a broth and is often served in a crab shell. The name is believed to come from cioppino, a classic Italian soup from Liguria, a region in Italy, that uses less tomato in the broth. Some versions include wine in the broth.

The earliest printed mention of the soup being called Cioppino in the United States may be that of a recipe in the 1906 "The Refugee's Cookbook." The cookbook was designed to serve as a fundraiser for the victims of the 1906 earthquake and fire in San Francisco that left were displaced after 80% of the city was destroyed.

We also ordered their Steamed Mussels with fennel, leeks, turmeric, white wine & grilled sourdough, $23. I first had this dish in Paris after my revival meeting there and fell in love. Years later Stephen and I backpack across Europe after he graduated from High School and we ate this dish at Leon Restaurant several times. This one was bit too saucy but still very good. I think we will be visiting the Small Batch every time we come to New York.

This sign was at our hotel room. I guess since New York legalized marijuana they have to post this. This really is a symbolic sign of our time.

Based on the article on December 30, 2022, 'New York opens its first legal recreational marijuana dispensary,' The first legal dispensary for recreational marijuana in New York rung up its first sales on Thursday, opening up what is expected to be one of the country's most lucrative markets for cannabis — underscored by the dozens of unauthorized shops that have operated in the open for years. The widely anticipated opening of the first state-sanctioned dispensary, which is operated by the nonprofit Housing Works, paves the way for a string of openings expected in the coming months in New York. The state legalized recreational marijuana use in March 2021.

I feel so sorry for America! We are sinking very fast at this time!

1/24: My commentary on Genesis, Part III was published via Amazon today – PTL!

Commentary: Genesis, Part III Paperback
24, 2023
by Robert Oh (Author)

See all formats and editions

Kindle
$5.35

Paperback
—

You Earn 27 pts

Read with Our Free App

This commentary is the result of my first 'Discipleship Training Through Genesis Kim of Berendo Street Baptist Church in 1987. Since then using this material I t Discipleship training in 1988 with College department members and then seven Community Church.

Report incorrect product information.

I am so glad I am writing commentary of the entire Bible now.

My friend wrote on his Facebook wall: Fun history of the day.

Jonathan Edwards (1703-1758) translated his own Bible from Greek and Hebrew by hand. He never bound it and would carry loose sheets of it around to preach. (Many do not know that this was fairly common of pastors to translate their own Bible and approximately 50,000 English translations of the Bible have been completed). He led the way to the greatest revival in America called the Great Awakening. He died at 55 years old after a reaction from a vaccination (smallpox). In 2023 most Americans know little about the Bible but are experts when it comes to Professional Sports. (Sorry that last line was just a joke. It's probably not true! He He).

I am enclosing one chapter from my commentary below:

Genesis 22:9-19. Teleological suspension of the ethical moment in history!

9 And they came to the place which God had told him of; and Abraham built an altar there, and laid the wood in order, and <u>bound</u> Isaac his son, and laid him on the altar upon the wood.

New International Version
When they reached the place God had told him about, Abraham built an altar there and arranged the wood on it. He <u>bound</u> his son Isaac and laid him on the altar, on top of the wood.

New Living Translation
When they arrived at the place where God had told him to go, Abraham built an altar and arranged the wood on it. Then he <u>tied</u> his son, Isaac, and laid him on the altar on top of the wood.

Bound, Tied: וַיַּעֲקֹד (way·ya·ʻă·qōḏ). Conjunctive waw | Verb - Qal - Consecutive imperfect - third person masculine singular. Strong's 6123: To tie with thongs.

Cross References:
- Hebrews 11:17 - By faith Abraham, when he was tested, offered up Isaac on the altar. He who had received the promises was ready to offer his one and only son,

- James 2:21 - Was not our father Abraham justified by what he did when he offered his son Isaac on the altar?

Q: Have you tried to tie someone with a rope? How difficult was it? How difficult could have been for an old man to tie down a young man?

Calvin: And they came to the place. Moses purposely passes over many things, which, nevertheless, the reader ought to consider. When he has mentioned the building of the altar, he immediately afterwards adds, that Isaac was bound. But we know that he was then of middle age, so that he might either be more powerful than his father, or, at least, equal to resist him, if they had to contend by force;

wherefore, I do not think that force was employed against the youth, as against one struggling and unwilling to die: but rather, that he voluntarily surrendered himself.zx

10 And Abraham stretched forth his hand, and took the knife to <u>slay</u> his son.

Aramaic Bible in Plain English
And Abraham reached his hand and he took the knife to <u>slaughter</u> his son.
Brenton Septuagint Translation
And Abraam stretched forth his hand to take the knife to <u>slay</u> his son.

Slaughter: לִשְׁחֹט (liš·ḥōṭ). Preposition-l | Verb - Qal - Infinitive construct. Strong's 7819: To slaughter, beat.

Calvin: The simplicity of the narrative of Moses is wonderful; but it has greater force than the most exaggerated tragical description. The sum of the whole turns on this point; that Abraham, when he had to slay his son, remained always like himself; and that the fortitude of his mind was such as to render his aged hand equal to the task of offering a sacrifice, the very sight of which was enough to dissolve and to destroy his whole body.

11 And the <u>angel</u> of the LORD called unto him out of heaven, and said, Abraham, Abraham: and he said, Here am I.

Literal Standard Version
And the <u>Messenger</u> of YHWH calls to him from the heavens and says, "Abraham, Abraham"; and he says, "Here I [am]";

New American Bible
But the <u>angel</u> of the LORD called to him from heaven, "Abraham, Abraham!" "Here I am," he answered.

Angel: מַלְאַךְ (mal·'aḵ). Noun - masculine singular construct. Strong's 4397: A messenger, of God, an angel.

Q: Soren Kierkegaard calls this moment 'Teleological suspension of the ethical.' Why?

Calvin: And the angel of the Lord called unto him. The inward temptation had been already overcome, when Abraham intrepidly raised his hand to slay his son; and it was by the special grace of God that he obtained so signal a victory.

12 And he said, Lay not thine hand upon the lad, neither do thou any thing unto him: for now I know that thou fearest God, seeing thou hast not withheld thy son, thine only son from me.
New American Standard Bible
He said, "Do not reach out your hand against the boy, and do not do anything to him; for now I know that you fear God, since you have not withheld your son, your only son, from Me."

NASB 1995
He said, "Do not stretch out your hand against the lad, and do nothing to him; for now I know that you fear God, since you have not withheld your son, your only son, from Me."

Cross References:
* James 2:21, 22 - Was not our father Abraham justified by what he did when he offered his son Isaac on the altar? You see that his faith was working with his actions, and his faith was perfected by what he did.

Pulpit Commentary: And he said, Lay not thine hand upon the lad, neither do thou any thing unto him. Abraham's surrender of the son of his affections having been complete, there was no need to push the trial further. The voice from heaven has been accepted as evidence of God's rejection of human sacrifices (Lange, Murphy), only that is not assigned as the reason for Isaac's deliverance. For now I knew - literally, have known; not caused thee to know (Augustine), but caused others to know (Lange); or the words are used anthropomorphically (Calvin) - that thou fearest God, - Elohim; the Divine intention being to characterize the patriarch as a God-fearing man, and not simply as a worshipper of Jehovah (cf. Quarry 'on Genesis,' p. 460) - seeing - literally, and (sc. in proof thereof) - thou hast not withheld thy son, thine only son from me. Καὶ οὐκ ἐφείσω τοῦ υἱοῦ σοῦ ἀγαπητοῦ δε ἐμέ (LXX.). Cf. ὅς γε τοῦ ἰδίου υἱοῦ οὐκ ἐφείσατο (Romans 8:32), as applied to the sacrifice of Christ. In this verse the angel of Jehovah identifies himself with Elohim.

13 And Abraham lifted up his eyes, and looked, and behold behind him a <u>ram</u> caught in a thicket by his horns: and Abraham went and took the ram, and offered him up for a burnt offering in the stead of his son.

Aramaic Bible in Plain English
And Abraham lifted his eyes, and he saw and behold, one ram caught in the branches by his horns, and Abraham went and he took the ram and offered him up as an offering in place of his son.

Brenton Septuagint Translation
And Abraam lifted up his eyes and beheld, and lo! a ram caught by his horns in a plant of Sabec; and Abraam went and took the ram, and offered him up for a whole-burnt-offering in the place of Isaac his son.

Ram: אַיִל ('a·yil). Noun - masculine singular. Strong's 352: Strength, strong, a chief, a ram, a pilaster, an oak, strong tree.

Ellicott's Commentary for English Readers: A burnt offering in the stead of his son.--We have here the fact of substitution, and the doctrine of a vicarious sacrifice. The ram took Isaac's place, and by its actual death completed the typical representation of the Saviour's death on Calvary. In The Speaker's Commentary it has been well shown, that there is no difficulty in this representation being composed of two parts, so that what was wanting in Isaac should be supplied by the ram. And while it would have been most painful for Isaac to have actually died by his father's hand, the doctrine of the possibility of a vicarious sacrifice would have been even less clearly taught thereby. He therefore rises again to life from the altar, and the ram dies in his stead, and by the two combined the whole mystery is set forth of God giving His Son to die for mankind, and of life springing from His death. Compare the mystery of the two birds, Leviticus 14:4; and the two goats, Leviticus 16:8.

14 And Abraham called the name of that place Jehovahjireh: as it is said to this day, In the mount of the LORD it shall be seen.

NASB 1977
And Abraham called the name of that place The LORD Will Provide, as it is said to this day, "In the mount of the LORD it will be provided."

Amplified Bible
So Abraham named that place The LORD Will Provide. And it is said to this day, "On the mountain of the LORD it will be seen and provided."

The LORD: | יְהוָה (Yah·weh). Noun - proper - masculine singular. Strong's 3068: LORD -- the proper name of the God of Israel.

Will Provide: יִרְאֶה (yir·'eh). Noun - proper - masculine singular Strong's 7200: To see.

Ellicott's Commentary for English Readers: Jehovah-jireh.--That is, Jehovah will provide. In Genesis 22:8, Abraham had said "Elohim-jireh," God will provide. He now uses Jehovah as the equivalent of Elohim. It is added that hence arose a proverb "In the mount of the Lord it shall be seen," or rather, In the mount of Jehovah it shall be provided.--The verb literally means to see, or, to see to a thing, and the sense of the proverb plainly is that in man's necessity God will Himself see to it, and provide due help and deliverance. The Samaritan, Syriac and Vulg. have a better reading, namely, "In the mount Jehovah will provide." This makes no change in the consonants, which alone are authoritative, but only in the vowels, which were added since the Christian era, and represent the tradition of the Jewish school of Tiberias. The LXX., without changing the vowels, translate, "In the mount Jehovah shall be seen," which would be a prophecy of the manifestation of Christ. The other two renderings, besides their general proverbial sense, point onward to the providing upon this very spot of the sacrifice that was to take away the sins of the world (comp. Isaiah 53:5).

Calvin: And Abraham called the name of that place. He not only, by the act of thanksgiving, acknowledges, at the time, that God has, in a remarkable manner, provided for him; but also leaves a monument of his gratitude to posterity. In most extreme anxiety, he had fled for refuge to the providence of God; and he testifies that he had not done so in vain. He also acknowledges that not even the ram had wandered thither accidentally, but had been placed there by God. Whereas, in process of time, the name of the place was changed, this was done purposely, and not by mistake. For they who have translated the active verb, He will see,' passively, have wished, in this manner, to teach that God not only looks upon those who are his, but also makes his help manifest to them; so that, in turn, he may be seen by them. The former has precedence in order; namely, that God, by his secret providence, determines and ordains what is best for us; but on this, the latter is suspended; namely, that he stretches out his hand to us, and renders himself visible by true experimental tokens.

15 And the angel of the LORD called unto Abraham out of heaven the second time, 16 And said, By myself have I sworn, saith the LORD, for because thou hast <u>done</u> this thing, and hast not withheld thy son, thine only son: 17 That in blessing I will bless thee, and in multiplying I will multiply thy seed as the stars of the heaven, and as the sand which is upon the sea shore; and thy seed shall possess the gate of his enemies;

New International Version
The angel of the LORD called to Abraham from heaven a second time and said, "I swear by myself, declares the LORD, that because you have <u>done</u> this and have not withheld your son, your only son, I will surely bless you and make your descendants as numerous as the stars in the sky and as the sand on the seashore. Your descendants will take possession of the cities of their enemies,

New Living Translation

Then the angle of the LORD called again to Abraham from heaven."This is what the LORD says: Because you have <u>obeyed</u> me and have not withheld even your son, your only son, I swear by my own name that I will certainly bless you. I will multiply your descendants beyond number, like the stars in the sky and the sand on the seashore. Your descendants will conquer the cities of their enemies.

Done, Obyed: עָשִׂיתָ ('ā·śî·tā). Verb - Qal - Perfect - second person masculine singular. Strong's 6213: To do, make.

Cross References:

- Romans 4:13 - For the promise to Abraham and his offspring that he would be heir of the world was not given through the law, but through the righteousness that comes by faith.

- Romans 9:27 - Isaiah cries out concerning Israel: "Though the number of the Israelites is like the sand of the sea, only the remnant will be saved.

- Hebrews 6:14 - saying, "I will surely bless you and multiply your descendants."

- Hebrews 11:12 - And so from one man, and he as good as dead, came descendants as numerous as the stars in the sky and as countless as the sand on the seashore.

Calvin: And the angel of the Lord called unto Abraham. What God had promised to Abraham before Isaac was born, he now again confirms and ratifies, after Isaac was restored to life, and arose from the altar, -- as if it had been from the sepulcher, -- to achieve a more complete triumph.

Thy seed shall possess the gate of his enemies. He means that the offspring of Abraham should be victorious over their enemies; for in the gates were their bulwarks, and in them they administered judgment. Now, although God often suffered the enemies of the

Jews tyrannically to rule over them; yet he so moderated their revenge, that this promise always prevailed in the end.

18And in thy <u>seed</u> shall all the nations of the earth be blessed; because thou hast <u>obeyed</u> my voice.

NASB 1977
"And in your <u>seed</u> all the nations of the earth shall be blessed, because you have <u>obeyed</u> My voice."

Amplified Bible
Through your <u>seed</u> all the nations of the earth shall be blessed, because you have heard and <u>obeyed</u> My voice."

Offspring, Seed: בְזַרְעֲךָ (bə·zar·ʿă·ḵā). Preposition-b | Noun - masculine singular construct | second person masculine singular Strong's 2233: Seed, fruit, plant, sowing-time, posterity.

Obeyed: שָׁמַעְתָּ (šā·ma'·tā). Verb - Qal - Perfect - second person masculine singular. Strong's 8085: To hear intelligently.

Cross References:
- Matthew 1:1 - This is the record of the genealogy of Jesus Christ, the son of David, the son of Abraham:

- Acts 3:25 - And you are sons of the prophets and of the covenant God made with your fathers when He said to Abraham, 'Through your offspring all the families of the earth will be blessed.'

- Galatians 3:8 - The Scripture foresaw that God would justify the Gentiles by faith, and foretold the gospel to Abraham: "All nations will be blessed through you."

- Galatians 3:16 - The promises were spoken to Abraham and to his seed. The Scripture does not say, "and to seeds," meaning many, but "and to your seed," meaning One, who is Christ.

Cambridge Bible for Schools and Colleges: In thy seed - See note on Genesis 12:3. The words might be also rendered "by thy seed." Because thou hast obeyed - Lit. "because thou hast heard," or "listened to." God's word may be a sound which is not heard; or it may be a sound which is heard, but not listened to; or it may be a sound which is heard, listened to, and obeyed.

19 So Abraham returned unto his young men, and they rose up and went together to Beersheba; and Abraham dwelt at Beersheba.

English Standard Version
So Abraham returned to his young men, and they arose and went together to Beersheba. And Abraham lived at Beersheba.

Berean Standard Bible
Abraham went back to his servants, and they got up and set out together for Beersheba. And Abraham settled in Beersheba.

Q: Imagine their trip back home of 3 days? How would it different than their prior jouney?

Calvin: And they rose up, and went together to Beer-sheba. Moses repeats, that Abraham, after having passed through this severe and incredible temptation, had a quiet abode in Beersheba. This narration is inserted, together with what follows concerning the increase of Abraham's kindred, for the purpose of showing that the holy man, when he had been brought up again from the abyss of death, was made happy, in more ways than one. For God would so revive him, that he should be like a new man.

20 And it came to pass after these things, that it was told Abraham, saying, Behold, Milcah, she hath also born children unto thy brother Nahor; 21 Huz his firstborn, and Buz his brother, and Kemuel the father of Aram, 22 And Chesed, and Hazo, and Pildash, and Jidlaph, and Bethuel.

American Standard Version
And it came to pass after these things, that it was told Abraham, saying, Behold, Milcah, she also hath borne children unto thy brother Nahor: Uz his first-born, and Buz his brother, and Kemuel the father of Aram, and Chesed, and Hazo, and Pildash, and Jidlaph, and Bethuel.

Aramaic Bible in Plain English
And it happened after these matters and it was shown to Abraham and they said to him, "Behold, Melka also gave birth to children by Nakhor your brother; To Uuts, his first born, and to his brother Buuz, and to Qemuyel, the father of Aram. And to Kasar, and to Khazu, and to Palrash, and to Yarlaph and to Bethuyel,

Pulpit Commentary: Verse 22. - And Chesed, - according to Jerome the father of the Chasdim or Chaldees (Genesis 11:28); but more generally regarded as the head of a younger branch or offshoot of that race (Keil, Murphy, Lange; cf. Job 1:17) - and Hazo, and Pildash, and Jidlaph (concerning whom nothing is known), and Bethnel - "man of God" (Gesenius); dwelling of God (Furst); an indication probably of his piety.

23 And Bethuel begat Rebekah: these eight Milcah did bear to Nahor, Abraham's brother. 24 And his concubine, whose name was Reumah, she bare also Tebah, and Gaham, and Thahash, and Maachah.

New International Version
Bethuel became the father of Rebekah. Milkah bore these eight sons to Abraham's brother Nahor. His concubine, whose name was Reumah, also had sons: Tebah, Gaham, Tahash and Maakah.

New Living Translation
(Bethuel became the father of Rebekah.) In addition to these eight sons from Milcah, Nahor had four other children from his concubine Reumah. Their names were Tebah, Gaham, Tahash, and Maacah.

38

Calvin: Moses also records the progeny of Nahor, but for another reason; namely, because Isaac was to take his wife from it. For the mention of women in Scripture is rare; and it is credible that many daughters were born to Nahor, of whom one only, Rebekah, is here introduced. He distinguishes the sons of the concubine from the others; because they occupied a less honorable place. Not that the concubine was regarded as a harlot; but because she was an inferior wife, and not the mistress of the house, who had community of goods with her husband. The fact, however, that it entered into Nahor's mind to take a second wife, does not render polygamy lawful; it only shows, that from the custom of other men, he supposed that to be lawful for him, which had really sprung from the worst corruption.

Daily Gospel Question: Have you ever experienced such 'Teleological suspension of the ethical' moment in order to obey God?

1/25: Jenny to Cambodia
Jenny had to go to Cambodia first before me since Oasis House needs their fearless leader to come back and start 2023 – giving them  direction and leadership. After dropping her off at LAX airport I met up with Dean, my Junior High and High School buddy, who is in charge of train system connecting LA Metro to LAX. Almost 50 years of friendship! He is planning to build his retirement home in Maui, so I told him to build a guest room! ☺ I guess our friendship will last life time! PTL!

1/27: Ttk Kamsa Church Friday Night revival.
'Ttk Kamsa' means 'Thanks again' in Korean. It was wonderful to fellowship with Pastor Ken Cho and ministered to his church again. He has been another 'Lifer' in my spiritual journey – thank God for friends like him.

They are making a plan to relocate their building again due to high rent in LA. I pray that God will lead and guide them to the perfect location where their people will grow and thrive in Jesus Name. Amen!

1/28: Go & Disciple Church of Orange County

I met Pastor John Park at HYM revival meeting ten year ago. He was a single man at that time and introduced his fiancée and asked for prayer. Now they have two children and serve the Lord joyfully together. It's so good to see young people pursuing God and His calling in their lives. Thank you Jesus!

1/29: Catalyst Church Sunday - Preaching again for Catalyst!

I was so happy to be able to minister to our church people again before going to Cambodia. Catalyst Church has become our home church in USA for Jenny and I. We love our small group brothers and sisters who are so faithful in praying for us – they are our biggest cheerleaders! Thank you BIG GOD small group!

1/29: Pastor Cho Jihoon of Korea is leading a revival meeting at Grace Mission International Church of Fullerton.

I met him last year in April in Korea. He is 12 years younger than me but he is so mature and deep in his understanding of the Gospel. I learn so much from him every time we meet. Thank you Jesus for friendship with such a great spiritual leaders of Korea! I am scheduled to minister to his people in Korea in February. Excited to see him in Korea again.

1/30-31: Robert to Korea

My flight from Los Angeles at 10:50AM on Monday, after 13 hours flight, I will arrive at Inchon, Korea at 5:40PM on Tuesday. I lose 17 hours of my life on this flight. Who says there is no such thing as 'Time Travel' – I do it all the time! ☺

My January Schedule page as an art form: This may become a collector's item 100 years later!

February

2/1: Day of Rest – Skyland Sauna experience
I love Korean Saunas – especially on a cold day like today.   What a treat to be able to relax and spend several hours in a hot bath and Jim Jil Pang! God is so good!

2/3: Seoul Grace Church – Meeting Pastor Kim.

I had a revival meeting scheduled at Ha Nam City. When I looked up the map, the Seoul Grace Church was literally walking distance from where I was holding the meeting. I called up Pastor Kim and had a wonderful fellowship and coffee! Seoul Grace Church is part of Grace Mission International of Fullerton, USA. GMI was founded as a church in support of world missions and today serves 307 missionaries in 59 different nations.

2/3-5: Revival meeting at SaeRom Church with Pastor Yom.

I met Pastor Yom at Berendo Baptist Church in Los Angeles in 1986.   She served as a children's minister and I was in charge of English ministry and Korean college group.   After completing her education, she came back to Korea and ended up planting a church at Ha Nam City.

I love this church full of young people. Some of them escorted me to a morning walk and then to a fantastic brunch! I ended up preaching one hour per session and many have received a gift of tongue at the end of our service. God is so good!

2/5-6: Sejong City visit with Pastor Lee Changwoo & Pastor Tim Park. I travelled to Sejong City again to meet up with Pastor Lee Changwoo and Pastor Tim Park.

1/6: Auntie Suh Jung Yeon at Pyong Tak.

Auntie Suh Jung Yeon is an angel for our family. She took care of our Mom until she passed away. She lived at her small apartment and fed her three times a day with healthy food and loved my Mom like a daughter! We are so thankful for her. When I found out that she lived at a city near Sejong City, I made a quick visit - sharing a meal and coffee. It was so sweet. When we saw each other we held each other's hand and wept – both missing our Mom.

2/7: HIPM (Healing Intercessory Prayer Ministry) special testimony meeting. I thank God for these intercessors who prayed for Jenny and I for literally few decades. They also open up their center for us every time we visit Korea. I hold a special teaching session for them and they prepare a feast for us. Hallelujah!

Pastor Lee Changwoo of Sejong City visited me at HIMP Center, because he was holding a lecture in the city. He is so well versed in Soren Kierkegaard's teaching, we have fantastic time sharing about how we can train the next generation Korean Christians with Kierkegaard's philosophy!

2/8: Eland Clinic Physical Check-up.
I tried to get physical check up once a year. Due to Covid-19 it wasn't possible for last three years. Finally I had chance to get it this

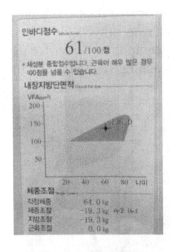

EE E·land Clinic
이랜드재단 이랜드의원

year at Eland Clinic. Eland is a Christian owned company that runs it's own clinic for its employees, but gives wonderful discount for pastors and missionaries. It used to be $150 for a complete check up but the fee went up to $250 this year, but still I get the complete check up within 3 hours with the printed results and a docotor's consultation at the end.

Bad news this year is that my test score was at 61 pts – I guess that would be D- if it was a standard test. Bascially the test results indicates that I need to lose 19.3 kg or 42 lbs ASAP. I have more fat that I need and I need more muscles than fat at this point.

Lord I need to stop eating and exercise more! I will take care of this body (only one) that you gave me!

2/8: Meeting Brother Andrew Lee of Interserve.
The perk of traveling is that you get to meet peole you want to meet. There are those you need to meet and there are those you want to mee. Brother Andrew is a friend you WANT to meet! Both he and I rode subway for one hour to see each other for about one hour of talk at coffee shop but it was totally worth it. PTL!

2/8: Meeting Brother Sam Son.

Brother Sam posted on his Face Book: 'It was a great privilege to catch up with Dr. Bob Oh during his visit to Korea. Having Northern Korean style dinner; Pyongyang Nangmyeon and Eobokjanban.'

It wasn't a meal, but an experience! Prayed for him since he's been having weird physical challenges. I told him, "You are too young to be sick!"

2/8: Pastor Eddie at Seoul University Hospital.

I saw this post by my friend Pastor Ryan Chang and found out our friend Pastor Eddie is in Korea getting the treatment for his advanced stage stomach cancer.

I make appointment with him and took taxi to see him so I can just pray for him. Lord will heal him and send him back to his church in Jesus Name. Amen! Pastor

Eddie is also too young to be sick like that. I am holding him and his health in my intercession. He wanted to take a photo with me but I refused – but told him that we will take a photo when he is completely healed and he looks his best! Lord let that day come sooner than later!

2/9: Pastor Pang's team – Lee family

My spiritual mentor Pastor Pang passed away several years ago, but I am still part of a team that tries to honour him and remember him by publishing his books into English. He left us with 103 books, we are trying to do at least 10 first. This beautiful couple have been spear heading the work faithfully! It was a wonderful Dim Sum experience as well. PTL!

2/9-10: Visiting City of Yangjoo and Jesus Power Church with Pastor Ryu.

This big man kidnapped me several years ago to his church at Yangjoo city claiming that I was their revival speaker for few years through my YouTube video. We became such a good friend, I try to visit his church each year when I am visiting Korea.

It is a small church with young people, but they are disciples of Christ who want to make difference in the world that they live in. Hallelujah!

2/9: Paul & Susan of China.

I first met them several years ago at Chiang Mai, Thailand. They lived in Irvine USA but ever since they became missionaries to China, they faithfully served the Lord abroad. Paul was diagnosed with cancer and now lives at Yangjoo city for treatment and recovery. My sister Somi wanted to support them so I was a delivery boy but enjoyed listening to their incredible testimony. God is good! Pray that God will also heal him completely in Jesus Name. Amen.

2/10: Agapao Friday night Revival.

Agapao Worship Team's Webpage states that they worships God in spirit and truth to open the gate of heaven and bring down the presence of the Holy Spirit. In every worship service, we praise and proclaim according to the heart that is given to us, and worship so that God's grace can be poured out more powerfully during sermon and prayer.

Hallelujah! We welcome you to the Agapao website in the name of the Lord. Agapao Ministry was created in 2012 starting with the employee Wednesday service. We experience healing and restoration by the grace of our Lord, revival and freedom of those who are oppressed, and especially the arising of Christians who have the Father's heart to take role of becoming the light and salt in the world, in their respective areas of business, entertainment, and media.

In addition, our ministry is to spread the flames of worship in Central Asia, the United States, Japan, C, R countries and more, with the desire to recover the Tabernacle of David within all nations. The vision of Agapao Ministry is to deliver God's love by caring for the poor and isolated, giving their needs, and to feed, clothe, save, raise up and send God's children all over the nation until the year of the Lord's favor is proclaimed.

I preached out of Luke 9:23 – Take up your cross daily and follow Jesus! We had the Holy Spirit fire anointing and we party till 1AM. Wow! PTL!

2/11-13: Retreat with Suwon Hana Church clusters.

When Pastor Koh contacted me about leading this revival retreat he asked me to preach minimum 90 minutes per session four times! What kind of request is that? But once I met more than thousand participants from 7 Hana Baptist Churches all over Korea I understood 'why' such request was made. They were so hungry for God and His Words – I ended up teaching 100 minutes per session. At the end of two days, Pastor Koh invited those who want to give their life as a full time ministers or missionaries, more than 100 came forward and received prayer. It was truly a revival time! Thank you Jesus!

2/13-14: Visiting city of Joomoonjin – Oh Kunteak family.

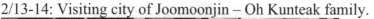

After such an intense weekend, I took KTX (Bullet train) to Joomoonjin and had a sashimi feast at Youngjin Sashimi restaurant. We met 10 years ago, and became friends for life. These are the folks I want to meet, not need to – so we have genuine care and love for each other; PTL! It was a very short but wonderful rest from very intense ministry weekend in Seoul and Suwon.

2/15: Pipe Gallery – Meeting Will & Mina.

I love art! Because I am an artist! Jenny still asks me, "What kind of art do you do?" Well, LIFE! To me to live is an act of art! I had such a wonderful time with Professor Jung Sungyoon who was doing a solo exhibit at Pipe Gallery. We discussed about how he wants to see reality beyond all that is visible and I prayed for his back since he was suffering from back pain! He is at the far right in the photo.

Afterwards, Will and his wife Mina had a wonderful Korean meal. They owned this gallery and wants to promote up and coming Korean artists in Korea and then abroad. They already made several local artists to become visible in USA art scene. PTL!

2/16: Suwon Hana EM Campus Outreach with Pastor Eljah Han. It was time of teaching and praying for people – many received fresh anointing from God. PTL!

2/17: Meeting Nancy Nunim of Mongolia

My sister Nancy couples was visiting Korea from Mongolia on her way to visit her daughter Jessica who just gave a birth to her second child. I was so happy that we can meet for lunch before I go to preach at Joyful Church that same evening! Auntie treated us with Seafood noodle at a specialty restaurant and had wonderful coffee afterwards. Life is good in Korea! But it was too cold for me. I start missing Cambodia and my favorite wife in Cambodia!

2/17: Meeting Pastor Singer Noah at Ilsan City.

I was able to meet Pastor Noah literally 500 meters away from Joyful Church as he was holding a concert at this beautiful boutique café. He is a non-resident missionary to Cambodia and we worked together for quite some time now. I was part of his mini-concert last year at Cambodia. God is so amazing!

2/17-18: Revival meeting at Joyful Church with Pastor Cho Jihoon.

I held three different meetings for this church. Friday night revival service for all the church members.

Then Saturday afternoon leadership meeting for all the leaders of the church. I spoke 2 and ½ hours nonstop! It was crazy intense but received well by all the participants. PTL!

Then we had Karis Academy's Book Publication celebration meeting with Pastor Lee Changwoo.

Pastor Lee Changwoo did a superb job of informing and inspiring all the participants to read Soren Kierkegaard more seriously and apply his teaching into our lives. I was so happy to be there and learn from the master!

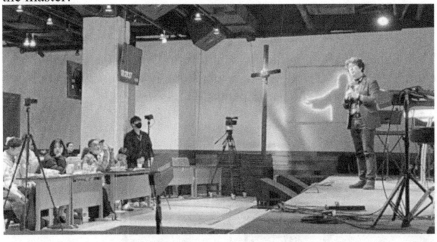

2/19: Inchon Grace Russian Church
Sister Inna was my translator at Grace Moscow Bible College in 2000. She now pastors a church for Russians with her husband Dimitry in Inchon, Korea.

It was wonderful to reconnect with Pastors Inna & Dimitri who's doing a great job of raising young Russian people to serve God in Korea. A brother who drove me to Seoul couldn't stop giving testimony about how his life was transformed by God and discipled by this wonderful couple – PTL!

2/19: Solomon's Porch Korea Church.

It feels so good to be among the kindred spirits! I was part of Hong Kong, Singapore, Shanghai, Beijing and now Korea Solomon's Porch. It is not the English language that brings us together, but the Spirit of Jesus make us a family of God. They had a wonderful dinner planned for me, but after 10 revival meetings in 21 days, I had to go back to HIPM Center and rest before taking off to Cambodia next day.

2/21: Arriving at Cambodia!

Due to delay at the Inchon airport I arrived at Phnom Penh at 1 AM. But I did not worry! My younger brother Daroth was waiting for me at the airport ready to take me home to Arata Oasis House. We met 15 years ago and he has been my faithful friend and TukTuk driver! Thank you Daroth!

2/22: Timothy Mission Center Opening Celebration.

I met Pastor Kim 22 years ago at Kampong Cham. He later comes to Fuller Theological Seminary and finishes his Doctor of Mission and offered a position as a senior pastor of an immigrant church in Los Angeles area. But he refused to settle at USA and chose to come back to Cambodia. I really respect him for that. It was such a wonderful occasion to celebrate his mission center today. Hallelujah!

Robert Oh
5d ·

Came back to Cambodia and attended Timothy Center Opening Ceremony: 디모데 선교 센터 헌당 감사 예배. Feb. 22, 2023. (9 Minutes video). Enjoy!!

YOUTUBE.COM
Timothy Center Opening Ceremony: 디모데 선교 센터 헌당 감사 예배. Feb. 22, 2023.

2/23: Pastor Steve Kang and his crew from USA
Pastor Steve from USA brought his short term mission team to support Brother Joseph Hwa who started serving at Cambodia last year. It's so good to see young people turned on to missional life!

Robert Oh
4d · 🔒

Wonderful lunch with Joseph Hwa and Pastor Steve and his crew from USA @ Aeon Mall II, Cambodia!

2/24: Jenny to Vietnam

Robert Oh
3d · 🔒

Jenny is leaving to Vietnam for a conference. I am home alone again! 😢

👍😮 Samin Lee, Yon Hui Kim and 167 others   26 comments

Jenny left me and went to Vietnam to attend her Women's Conference. How sad! I made a 50 second video of her departure and me crying. ☺

167 of my Face Book friends thought it was cute!

2/24: Zoom meeting with BIG GOD small group of Catalyst Church. It was so much fun to be with loved ones of Catalyst Church. I was really getting into sharing then 'BAM' the electricity goes out. We

59

did not have such rolling black out for awhile, but during our zoom meeting it happens. It is this sort of episode reminds me that I am still at a mission field!

2/27: First day of lecture at CPTI – Cambodia Presbyterian Theological Institute.

I have two classes to teach this time in Cambodia: Research Method and Christian Life by Pastor Pang.

It was so good to go bit early and witness all the students crying out to God in prayer during their afternoon chapel.

I have 3 hours lecture for Th. M. students – that's Master of Theology courses.

I am so happy that I have such privilege to share my life experience with next phase Chrisitan leaders of Cambodia. Thank you, Jesus!

ជីវិតគ្រីស្ទបរិស័ទ

បកប្រែដោយ លោកគ្រូ ប៉ាង ពិភព្វ

I had Pastor Steve Kang translate Pastor Pang's book 'The Christian Life' into English and then two years ago translated into Khmer. After almost one and half year of review and revision, it is finally available. We still have to publish with CPTI publishing department, but at least all of my students and read this book in Khmer – PTL!

2/28: Open House dinner at Brother Nit's.

We met 15 years ago at Center of Peace and all of them still love Jesus and love us! What JOY we have in Jesus. Thank you Lord for these wonderful disciples of Christ who's making impact and following you in Cambodia. PTL!

My February Schedule page as an art form: This may become a collector's item 100 years later!

March

3/1-14: 14 Days Fasting - Food, Coffee & Media (21 days) Fasting.

According to Deborah Weatherspoon, "About 75 to 80 percent of people in the world drink caffeinated beverages regularly. In the United States, the amount of caffeine intake increases by age, peaking in the 50 to 64 age group. Coffee is the main source of caffeine, followed by carbonated soft drinks and teas. All of that caffeine can lead to caffeine dependency. Although it's hard to pinpoint an exact number of how many people have caffeine dependency, studies indicate that more than a quarter of people who use caffeine met the criteria listed on the Diagnostic and Statistical Manual of Mental Disorders (DSM-5) Substance Dependence list. If you drink coffee or beverages that contain caffeine every day, you may suffer from caffeine withdrawal symptoms."[1]

And boy did I have a major caffeine withdrawal this time! According to Deborah's report, "There are also physical symptoms of caffeine withdrawal. According to some research, by far the most common symptom is headache, but other symptoms of withdrawal include:

- fatigue
- low energy and activeness
- decreased alertness
- drowsiness
- overall "bad mood" and discontent
- depressed mood
- difficulty concentrating
- irritability
- feeling foggy

---

[1] https://www.healthline.com/health/caffeine-withdrawal. Accessed on 30 Mar. 2023.

The physical effects of caffeine withdrawal can also include flu-like symptoms like nausea, vomiting, and muscle pain or stiffness."[2] And I had all of the above symptoms! I decided to cut back on my coffee consumption and go on to coffee fast time to time so I won't be dependent on coffee anymore. Thank you Lord for this lesson this time of fast.

3/6: CPTI Lecture on The Christian Life - 2:30 to 5:30 PM *Every Monday in March.

This was my 6th day of fasting, and I had to teach 3 hours lectures. To say the least, it wasn't easy but it wasn't impossible. It's usually like this, what seems impossible to accomplish, once you start at it, you can manage to finish.

3/7: CPTI Lecture on Research Method - 8:30 - 11:30 AM *Every Tuesday in March.

Today was even more challenging, especially I was still going through caffeine withdrawal symptoms.

3/9: Commentary: Genesis, Part IV was published in America via Amazon. PTL!

Look inside ↓

Commentary: Genesis, Part IV Paperback – March 9, 2023

by Robert Oh (Author)

New to Amazon

See all formats and editions

Kindle	Paperback
$5.35	$9.00
You Earn: 27 pts	You Earn: 18 pts prime
Read with Our Free App	1 New from $9.00

Kindle Rewards Beta

Earn Kindle Points, get Kindle book credit

Earn Kindle Points when you buy books. Redeem for Kindle book credit. Learn more.

---

[2] Ibid.

I am always so amazed at amount of time you have when you fast food and media for long time. You become so productive each day for having 3-4 extra hours a day.

3/14: 28 Days of Miracle is published.
This book started out as a passing thought in Korea! What can God do in 28 days with an average guy like me who is passionate about serving our Lord Jesus Christ? It's all about God and our Lord Jesus, and what one can do when he is empowered by Holy Spirit God's anointing. This is my testimony book.

I included some researched information about my experiences in Korea and Cambodia for the readers to experience and be more informed about the location and organizations I work with.

28 days by number:
- 12 Cities: Ministered.
- 12 revival or ministry meetings.
- 1 time Radio Interview at Far East Radio.
- 77 times: Preached and Lectured (Including YouTube teaching)
- 100 + pages written for the Commentary on Genesis.
- 4 times: Book Talk via YouTube and GBS Radio.
- 45 coffee tasting: Coffee Diary.

3/15: USA Short Term Mission Team (STM) arrives!

Ya Ya Sisters Mission Log: Arrival & Day 1. March 15 & 16, 2023.

Jenny invited 9 ladies from USA to help her with the Healing Enounter and Breakthrough conference and they have come!!

3/16: Dino Café & Restaurant opens

Dino Cafe & Restaurant: WOW - Come and check this place out! 5 Star recommendation by Dr. Bob Oh!

I prayed to God when we moved in to Oasis House two year ago that we would have a café near by. Lord answered my prayer and within 50 steps of our place Dino Café started. Then Jenny prayed for a restaurant to start near by. Dino Café started to serve breakfast and lunch! How wonderful is that? I mad a video promo for them and they LOVED it! And we LOVED the fact that we can have Cambodian breakfast noodle anytime we want. All the Ya Ya Sisters from USA used this place as their breakfast place as well. God is so amazing!

3/17-18: Healing Encounter Meeting at Himawari Hotel with USA STM.

Oasis House Healing Encounter Conference 1: Introduction to Inner Healing. By: Jenny Oh. 3/17/23

Oasis House Healing Encounter Conference 1: Introduction to Inner Healing. By: Jenny Oh. 3/17/23

Oasis House invited 60 Cambodian counselors and Christian leaders to this conference and we had two days of Holy Spirit party! God moved so powerfully with all the speakers from both USA and Oasis House, that we could only credit God and give Him glory! PTL!

3/19: Worship service with Encounter House and USA STM.

It was wonderful time of intimate worship after such a large event at a hotel. At Oasis House our Encounter House Church met and had a great time of worship and fellowship. We learned that 'flexibility' is our friend and 'expectation' is our enemy! The one was scheduled to preach couldn't come and notified us night before. I had to step in and be flexible leader who can back up for a young leader! ☺

3/20: Trip to Kampong Cham with USA STM. *Jenny travels to Angkor Wat with USA STM team from there.

So good to be back at Galilee Church of Pumtrung, Kampong Cham!

It was so healing and redeeming for Jenny and I to visit this leprosy village again. Thank you Jesus!

We started a school near by from this village to isolate around 130 young people and started educating them since 2002. Then through some unfortunate turn of event we couldn't visit them for last 15 years. But through God's grace and supernatural favor we reconnected with them and were able to visit them with our USA team. PTL! God moved so powerfully through teaching, praying and home visitation – everyone were happy in the Lord! God is so good!

3/21: Logos School - Chapel for middle school and high school.

When I am asked to minister to young people – my answer is usually YES! I want to see young people get turned on to Christ. They would have their entire life to serve God and follow Jesus! This was

also no exception. Logos School asked me to lead both chapels for their middle school and high
School I said YES without any hesitation. All the missionaries and school staff work so hard to share the Gospel with these students, I wanted to do my part in blessing the young people of Cambodia as well. I found my friend Pastor Eric recommendation of this school at their website so included it here. And bit about Logos School as well.

 I can honestly say we could not be living and serving in Cambodia like we are today without the love and support Logos gives to our children. My wife and I have the utmost confidence in the administration, educators, and staff at Logos knowing that my children are getting an excellent education that is grounded deeply in the word of God. That kind of confidence is invaluable. It frees us up to live and serve in Cambodia knowing that our children are well taken care of. – Eric Beck.

Logos International School is a ministry of Asian Hope, which exists to reach Cambodia for Christ, largely by providing quality Christian education, to children of all socioeconomic levels. Logos is a fully-accredited member of both the Association of Christian Schools International (ACSI) and the Western Association of Schools and Colleges (WASC). Instruction is in English and follows an American curriculum. Logos has been reaccredited from July 1, 2022–June 30, 2028. The ACSI/WASC Visiting Team Report can be found here.

Though a Christian school, with a strong Christian mission, Logos welcomes students from all faiths and nationalities. The Logos student body consists largely of Cambodian children and children of missionaries from various countries. Some of the twenty-five nationalities represented at Logos include Cambodian, American, Korean, Chinese, Indonesian, Thai, Finnish, Canadian, Singaporean, Malaysian, and Australian.

Logos currently serves about 350 students, from PreK – 3 (three-year-olds) through 12th grade. Average class size is about 25. Our teachers are all native English speakers and largely from the United States or British Commonwealth countries. Each elementary grade also has at least one Khmer speaking Teaching Assistant. Logos School Profile.

The school also provides vibrant Arts and Physical Education programs, a professional Learning Support team, serving PreK to 12th grade, and an Interscholastic Athletics program for both girls and boys – basketball, volleyball & soccer. Logos' sister school under the Asian Hope organization is the Asian Hope International School, offering bilingual (Khmer/English) instruction, designed primarily to meet the educational needs of local Khmer students.

OUR MISSION: Logos International School is dedicated to academic excellence in providing a well-rounded, quality, Christian education to students from all ethnic and socioeconomic backgrounds. Upon graduation, students will be equipped to view all aspects of life from a biblical perspective, to serve and help transform their communities for Christ, and to pursue further education.

OUR VISION: Every student is a spiritually maturing, academically equipped, and socially responsible individual.

OUR MOTTO: A heart for Christ, for Truth, and for the World.

OUR EXPECTED SCHOOLWIDE LEARNING RESULTS (ESLRS)
Our goal is for every Logos graduate to exemplify the following:

1. A SPIRITUALLY MATURING INDIVIDUAL, WHO IS EQUIPPED TO —
- Has a growing relationship with Christ as his/her personal Saviour
- Finds his/her identity in Christ
- Appreciates the Bible as the inspired Word of God
- Participates in service and evangelism, and share and defend his/her beliefs

- Makes moral and ethical decisions based on a biblical worldview
- Recognizes the importance of a well-balanced spiritual, emotional, and physical lifestyle

2. AN ACADEMICALLY SOUND STUDENT, WHO IS —
- Equipped to achieve his/her God-given potential
- A rational and critical thinker, who applies understanding and knowledge to new problems
- Developing skills to be a lifelong learner
- An effective communicator in speech and writing
- Technologically literate and able to apply technology productively and ethically

3. A SOCIALLY RESPONSIBLE WORLD CITIZEN, WHO —
- Takes personal responsibility for actions and attitudes
- Recognizes and respects authority
- Has Christian love and compassion for people of all gender, races, backgrounds, and social status
- Exercises servant leadership with humility and integrity
- Is an effective team member
- Has an appreciation for culture and the arts
- Is a good steward of all that God has given us

3/21: CPTI & Bible School Fellowship joint meeting with 5 Bible Schools in Cambodia.

Although I couldn't attend this meeting due to conflict of my schedule, I thought this event was significant for me to report. I am so happy my school CPTI is hosting this unity rally of Cambodian future pastors!

3/21: Dinner with Cambodian Philosophers!

I taught a course on Metaphysics at RUPP six years ago and we still meet time to time to check up on each other! Our Socrates came back from Japan to do some research for his Master program for University of Hiroshima, we wanted to celebrate together.

3/22-24: Elder Hong's class on Songs of Solomon at Lucky International Hotel of Phnom Penh, Cambodia.

I am co-authoring a commentary on the Song of Solomon with Elder Steve Hong. This book is a result of two events taking place simultaneously in March 2023 at Phnom Penh, Cambodia.

First, Elder Steve Hong conducts 'The Spirituality of the Bride' seminar for Cambodian pastors and Korean missionaries on March 22 – 24, 2023. Second, I finished reading his commentary on the Song of Solomon and wrote my commentary on it as well. I decided to incorporate his teaching as the major component of my commentary along with the Matthew Poole's Commentary.

3/24: Chilling with Logos brothers!

Rule of thumb – Don't ever say NO to an offer to share a meal with cool brothers in Lord laboring at the mission field together. That's what happened today. I had to run to my next appointment after preaching at Logos

School, they wanted to treat me to a nice lunch later in the week. How can you say NO to that!
We had such a wonderful time of fellowship! Thank you guys for being part my journey in Cambodia. Next time it's my treat!

3/24: USA STM team fly back to USA.

These ladies were the power house team for Cambodia. I am so happy that Jenny invited them to Cambodia this year. It seems like it will be an annual event for Oasis House to host 'Healing Encounter and Breakthrough' Conference.

3/26: Preaching at the Timothy Center Church – Sunday Service.

Missionary Kim asked me causally, "So when are you coming to our church?" Hum, I did not know I had to go to his church? ☺ But I was happy that he asked me to come and share the message. I love these wonderful students at Timothy Center Church. They live together and attend colleges and experiencing Christian community.

I see them grow up physically and also spiritually maturing as a leaders! PTL!

3/26: Korea HIPM & Oh Family team from Korea arrives.

Jenny invited HIPM inner healing team and our Oh family from Joomoonjin to Cambodia to help out with her outreach ministry. We are enjoying a boat ride at Phnom Penh!

3/28: Takeo Kindergarten visit.

Missionary Yoo Jungmee opened this kindergarten at Takeo 16  years ago. WOW! These kids were so cute and we fell in love with them. We ended up holding each child and praying for them.

This is the best photo I took this year. Mrs. Oh was sincerely praying for a girl and I can feel the squeeze of Jesus' love from her! PTL!

3/29: Korean Missionary Association – 30th Anniversary celebration. I was asked to be the master of ceremony for this event to lead a panel of great Christian leaders of Cambodia. I was honored to be part of this monumental event for Korean missionaries.

3/30: Day of Reflection for the month of March 2023.
Oh family went back to Korea last night and HIPM team is ministering to many people at Oasis House. After one hour swim this morning, I am finishing my March report and will take off to a

half a day retreat to hide somewhere and talk to God! Life is really good here in Cambodia for me. How do I get to live such life! Thank you Lord!

3/31: My first Sprint Triathlon Finished! PTL!

Sprint Triathlon: Formally, a sprint distance triathlon consists of a 750m swim, a 20k bike, and a 5k run. If you look around your local scene you will find that many races will advertise varying race length distances for a "sprint" triathlon.

I have been training for it for such a long time. Yesterday I went to the Aeon Mall II and bought a bicycle and decided to go for it in the morning. Swimming was not a problem since I've been swimming 1 mile each day, but bicycling was tough. I need a better saddle! ☺ I had to walk most of my running portion, because my leg was wobbly by the time running segment came. But it's DONE! I am an official Triathlete!

3/31: Lunch with college buddies at Myonwolkwan, Phnom Penh.
It's amazing how 4 college buddies ended up at Cambodia! One of the best features of living in Cambodia is food is still reasonable. We had BBQ lunch special for $8 per person! You can't beat that!

This is Jenny's Quarterly report for Oasis House:

Oasis House 1st Quarter Report 2023
By Jenny Oh

Hello everyone, greetings in the Lord!

I am in Korea for a week before I get back to USA tomorrow as I write this report. It's been an amazing quarter. We had 9 people US team and 5 people Korean team back to back starting from March 15th through April 2nd. Last year, God gave me a heart to do a Healing Encounter Conference this spring and gave me two words: "Healing and Break through" based on Ephesians 3:16 and 19, to strengthening the Innerman, and to live a life of Fullness in God. I am convicted God will use Cambodia to evangelize Southeast Asia and beyond, and we need to be prepared for this outpouring of His Spirit, like the ten wise virgins.

I had no idea how it would be, but the team of 9 short term missionaries were all called to come to Cambodia by conviction, and they were all Inner Healers, and Intercessors. They also brought incredible and overwhelming resources that enabled us to do all the ministries without having to be limited in anyway. These are the ministries we were able to do within those two weeks:

- March 15 - USA team arrived.
- March 17-18 - Healing Encounter Conference: 60 people limit were quickly filled. It was held as two day conference at the Himawari Hotel.

- March 20 - Poum Trung Leper's Village Outreach: this is the first village Pastor Robert and I reached out to in 2001, our first ministry in Cambodia.
- March 21-23 - Healing Retreat: The short termers ministered to each other with inner healing and a wonderful time of rest in a resort hotel.
- March 26 - Korean team arrived.
- March 27 - Soccer Outreach to Inner City Poor children.
- March 28 - Ministry to Missionary Yoo's Kindergarten and the teachers with Inner Healing and prayer at a provence two hours away from Phnom Penh.
- March 29-30 - Individual Inner Healing sign ups for Korean women missionaries in Cambodia.

Needless to say it was a busy quarter but I felt the Lord's pleasure as I saw a vision of the "Fruitful Vine" as I wrapped up the ministry before leaving Cambodia to Korea. For the counseling ministry, from January to march, we had 169 cases including my 11 cases in USA. I've decided to hold office hours while in USA two and a half days a week, there's much need I'm discovering.

Praise Report
- We are beginning to see the signs of revival in Cambodia and people hungry for the things of the Spirit.
- Healing Encounter Conference was an amazing time for everybody; the participants as well as for the short term missions team: It was great to witness missionaries along side the Oasis House staff ministering effectively and with power through teaching, prayer and leading small groups. There were much testimonies after the conference.
- The short term missionaries testified break throughs in their own lives from their missions experience in Cambodia.
- As we ministered to the villages, we were experiencing the move of the Spirit as people were touched and received prayer.
- We set up Sand Tray Therapy Room and will be ministering to our young clients and those who has hard time expressing

through words. We will also be receiving supervision for this therapy. The 5 Staff and Volunteers successfully completed part A of PACT counseling training in Chiang Mai and will continue to be supervised and trained on line.

- Korean women missionaries are coming together and forming stronger connection through Oasis Ministry.
- Oasis was able to provide Health Insurance for the Staff due to generous donations from the short term missionaries.

Prayer Request
- As we invest our staff and volunteers in PACT, they will be well equipped and mature counselors.
- CWF Lay Counseling material to be well translated by the volunteers.
- We will be well prepared for another year of CWF Lay Counseling Training but this time in Khmer.
- Health of our staff and P. Oh and Jenny as we travel and minister.
- As we expand, we need more funding for our training and programs, pray that the Lord will amply provide. We are praying more churches and individuals can commit this year.
- Oasis House to be faithful in the leading of the Spirit to serve this country to bring healing and freedom.

Jenny Oh
Director
Oasis House

My March Schedule page as an art form: This may become a collector's item 100 years later!

April

4/1: Jenny - Korean Women's Healing Encounter Day at Oasis House.
Korean Women's Encounter day retreat: Around 17 missionaries and business women were ministered with teaching on inner healing, group and individual prayer time at Oasis House.

살아있는 나무 그리고
죽은 가지들:
내적 치유 이야기

Jenny Oh

They are using Jenny's book in Korean edition. Sarah Sung of Cambodia translated Jenny's book into Korean and Oasis House self-published at Phnom Penh using a local printing shop. The quality was acceptable and Jenny used her book as the main text for this retreat and everyone were so blessed by it. I have sent in the Korean manuscript to Kyu Jang Publishing House of Korea and waiting to see if they want to publish it. If not, most likely we will publish it under Karis Academy Publishing.

This small book is making a hugh impact – PTL!

4/2: Encounter House Sunday service at Oasis House.
Jenny and I are always amazed at the quality of our worship at Encounter House Sunday service. So few of us and yet we touch heaven every single time we get together. Thank you Jesus for your presence and anointing for this house church! Oasis House host our church once a month! Mrs. Kim from USA provided pizza lunch for everyone. Double blessing!

4/3: CPTI - 3 hours lecture on church planting examples. Missionary Yang's team – Thoun & Raksmey came and challenged our CPTI students to be planting self-sustainable churches in Cambodia.

My Th.M. student, Mourng Kakruna wrote the following report on Missionary Yang's presentation. He did an excellent job so I am sharing it here:

Title: Building A Self-Supporting Church in Cambodia
Question: What are the main missions of the church (Christian)?
1) Preach the gospel to unbelievers
2) Make(train) the believers to follow Jesus(disciples)

For me, both ministries are the most important thing in planting a church of God. I came to Cambodia to complete the mission and learned the Khmer language. Before I started planting the church, I did a lot of research on the streets and in the villages, and I also asked the villagers many questions related to the church planting in their village. At that time, I was considering the school, so I went to school, met with teenagers, and asked them questions about their interests and about what they wanted to learn. After doing research, I found a village called Kampong Por village, Kampong Phnom commune, Leuk Dek district.

 In 2008 we started teaching English classes. At that time, there was no electricity, no clean water in the village, and no rental house for foreigners, so we borrowed a small room size 2m x 3m to teach English to children and Korean to teenagers. Then we started to worship and preach the gospel, and there were so many people coming to join. But I had a question, how many years did I need to spend preaching the gospel to Cambodians? Preach the Gospel or educate the Gospel? It takes at least seven years for Cambodians to understand the Christian gospel. -Heng Chen-

Cambodians need to be educated about the gospel for seven years but not to believe, only to understand the gospel. Some people have been baptized, but not one hundred percent believe in Jesus, so they need more gospel education. Therefore, it takes a long time to help Cambodians truly believe in Jesus. Consequently, I used strategies:

The 1st strategy: Educating the gospel

Gospel education is different from evangelism. Evangelism is to meet people only once or twice, once a month or once a year, but the Gospel education is the same as the government school, it has to be met every day regularly. For Cambodians and teenagers, I met 15 years ago to believe in Jesus, I began educating them about the gospel. What must we do to educate the gospel? We worship at 5 am, and at 9 pm we worship again. Because by that time, there was no electricity and no clean water. Once the church was built, there was a light and clean bathroom at church, also they could eat noodles at night as well. At the church, at that time there was a generator, and we used it from 5 pm to 10 pm. Because they wanted to study, but there was no electricity in their house, so they came to church every day to study.

I also taught them about tithing, thanksgiving offering, and love offering. Tithing once a week and once a month. Teenagers had no salary, so they can tithe once a week, saving their daily allowance. I taught them a lot about tithe and offering. So, my first strategy is to educate the gospel not merely preach the gospel.

The 2nd strategy: sharing everything about the church with young leaders

I think there are not many believers in Cambodia from birth. Me, I believed in Jesus from birth because my parents were believers, my grandparents were believers, and my grandparents were also believers, so I knew a lot about Jesus. Cambodians believe in Buddhism from birth, so, to understand the gospel, I had to educate them on a lot of the gospel. Once they grew up and became leaders, I began teaching them everything. Every single day we had a meeting.

In particular, I taught about the use of budget. When guests from Korea, from the United States, donated $ 20,000 to the church, I met with young people and discussed how to use the money. Because the next time I will leave the church, so they have to learn to discuss how to use the money. Many years later, we found some people who could lead the church. This is the 2nd strategy.

The 3rd strategy: creating jobs for the young leaders

    I saw a problem through other missionaries. When the high school students finished school, they went to work in Phnom Penh. I have been trying to educate them for ten years, then after they graduate and leave for Phnom Penh. Establishing an early church requires a leader, so I created a job by opening a private school. to keep them from leaving. When the school first opened, there were only four students, but the number of students later increased. And two years ago, the church could stand on its own. The church can now stand on its own, governed by a pastor Thoun, and has committee discussions. On October 19, 2023, I will announce my resignation, hand over everything to the Cambodian people, and preach the gospel by themselves.

4/4: My Book Talk on Soren Kierkegaard's book in Korea is now posted at one of the leading Christian YouTube – Oh Kong Shin, meaning 'Today's Theological Study.'

키르케고르의 대표작, "복음과 함께 고난을 받으라" 북토크 | 카리스아카데미 북토크 Full Ver.

4/6: Jenny to Korea.

Jenny wanted to host Mrs. Kim to Korea trip. She will be staying at HIPM center with her and travel to USA with her. Jenny is being such a wonderful host and almost like a daughter to Mrs. Kim. Mrs. Kim came to Cambodia almost 15 times as a chief intercessors for all of our mission efforts. Praise the Lord for such a woman of faith in our lives.

4/7: One day retreat all by myself at Palace Gate Hotel.

I had to take one day off from my crazy schedule. Jenny and I found this boutique hotel by the river near Royal Palace called 'Palace Gate Hotel' and it has been our secret get away place. I rested and had a wonderful steak dinner all by myself! ☺

4/8: Thrive Conference – As a Panel speaker.

Martalia of ACTS recommended me as a speaker to 'Thrive Conference.' I wanted to see what others are doing on the issue of healing in Cambodia. Since it was not a Christian meeting, I was part of panel composed of secular Khmer leaders and a monk. I found following information on the conference - Thrive Conference: Courage to Dream 2023. Inspiring healing & thriving, minds & hearts of

Cambodia. Cambodia Coaching Institute is preparing to host its first-ever conference on mental health, which will highlight the significance of mental health in Cambodia's social and economic growth. The conference is set to take place on April 8, 2023, and will bring together policymakers, health professionals, and civil society organizations to discuss the importance of prioritizing mental health, reducing stigma, and increasing access to mental health services. The event aims to raise awareness and promote collaboration to improve mental health in Cambodia.

4/9: Children of Light Church Resurrection Sunday service leading with Pastor Joseph Lee of KIMNET, USA.

Pastor Joseph Lee of KIMNET came to Cambodia to be part of our conference. We enjoyed ministering for the Resurrection Sunday service. I donated Pastor Pang's book, 'The Christian Life' to them so they can use it for their discipleship training. PTL!

4/10: CPTI - 3 hours lecture on church planting examples.

Missionary Ji's team – Samnang & Cheata from Children of Light Church came and shared their work with CPTI students.

Keo Nang, one of my student, made following report on Missionary Ji's presentation as follows:

Missionary Ji arrived in Cambodia in 2008 and will continue his mission to God until 2023. He is currently the pastor of Children Of Light Church and has three sons and daughters.

Ji was sent by a church in South Korea to serve God in Cambodia. By sending a teacher for the relationship with students and also started that work at the Royal University of Phnom Penh. First, the teacher builds relationships with the students there, sometimes inviting them home to socialize. Sometimes it was not until 2009 that the teacher set up a dormitory for students to stay. At other times, through communication, the teacher also went on evangelistic missions in the provinces, especially in Kandal province.

Apart from the ministry in the province, Phnom Penh is also a special point, in the morning the teacher always trains the leaders to know about God. Through prayer, scripture study, etc. In my mind, I think that is the key to faith in the church, to build leaders, and growing the church.

Creating a Dorm: Another task is to create a dormitory for students from the province to stay in Phnom Penh to study, both for students of both sexes.

Creating a Cell Team: Dr. Chin thought that the church could only grow if the church could be strong enough to form a small group of leaders to make church grow. Each team with strong faith can continue to create new teams. While Covid 19 was under attack, they were still in harmony. Sometimes in small groups, there is worship, fellowship, prayer, and hearing. And also make this church grow more.

Ministries for Children and Children: For children, the ministry is designed for children whose parents are believers in God. Some of them are graduates of schools where alumni become leaders and they will stay there. The church and its members think that their children should study in church with the help of the pastor and receive the love of God that cannot separate them from God. The mission for the school is Shine School in Phnom Penh: In this school, there is a tutoring course for other students, that is, open classes for kindergarten students and a ministry for football teams.

Ministry for the provinces: In addition to the ministry for the gods in Phnom Penh, teachers continue to work for the gods in other provinces. Starting with students who have become special staff with Pastor Chhe Samnang and Teacher Sok Cheata.

1- Koh Chen
2- Udong
3- Third, Kampong Cham province

4/11: CPTI - 3 hours lecture on 'The Christian Life.' *Final Class

I shared my final CPTI class with Pastor David Bastes and had him share about our house church model to my students. It was so wonderful to see young pastors interacting one another wanting to see God's people trained and mobilized for church planting effort in Cambodia.

4/11: Check into the Garden City Hotel in preparation for KIMNET conference. Around 70 people from all over the world arrived at the hotel around midnight. Thank God none was lost!

4/12-15: KIMNET conference at Phnom Penh, Cambodia.

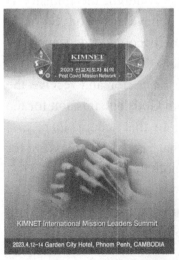

This conference was one of the most difficult one I had to organize. Many logistic issues went South real quickly and we had to come up with solution on the spot. For example, one of the participants booked the wrong flight and ended up and Saigon, Vietnam. She then took 6 hours bus ride to Phnom Penh and took a Grab Taxi and got lost around midnight near hotel. She called me panicking, "Where am I? There is nothing but a field and Taxi driver wants me to get out!" Hum… what would you do when you get call like that at midnight? God intervened and everyone eventually made to the conference and it ended with everyone 'happy' about the conference. I think this will be my last KIMNET conference. God spoke very clearly about launching KAGMA meetings from now on. Thank you Jesus!

4/14: Pastor Samuel Choe visits Oasis House & Cambodia Research and Resource Center.

I did not think we can host them because KIMNET conference schedule was so jammed packed, yet God allowed us to visit Oasis House during lunch break. Pastor Samuel came with Victoria SMN & Pastor Park John of SEED and prayed a prayer of blessing! This has been the highlight of April for me.

4/15: Donating Pastor Pang's book and Soren Kierkegaard book to

Jesuit Research Center in Phnom Penh. Father Kang was suffering from Dengue Fever but graciously hosted us and showed his research center and library to us. Missionary Dongkyu Kim never met Catholic priest before so it was wonderful time to share my good friend with him. He gave me his latest publication as well. PTL!

4/16: UBF Church of Cambodia worship service

Brother John Seo of UBF was one of the speaker at KIMNET meeting and he was leading a worship service for UBF Church of Phnom Penh. I wanted to experience their church planting effort and ended up having wonderful fellowship after the service. They church planting team members were all professionals and working and serving at that level, but discipling few college students and planted a house church model church. I think we can

94

learn from each other and share notes on church planting models in Cambodia.

4/16: Back to USA. I am finally back in USA. First thing I wanted to do was plant all kinds of vegetables at our backyard.

Unfortunately I pulled my back during leveling the ground and Jenny had to finish the work. We bought all kinds of plants – pepper, squash, zucchinis and cucumbers. Since we will be leaving to Cambodia end of July, it is crucial that we plant them ASAP.

I had to cancel my Sunday service session, because I was in so much pain. I think it was the first time that I cancel a Sunday service due to injury. Thank God for our acupuncturist, I was 80% healed by first session and 95% by second session the following Monday and Wednesday.

4/21: Lausanne 4 East Asia Zoom meeting.
The 4th Lausanne Conference will be held at Korea in 2024. You have to be invited to come to that conference. Thank God one of the PhD student at OCMS, whom I sort of helped in his PhD journey is in charge of East Asia. So I participated at their zoom meeting. I think I am invited to come next year. PTL!

4/24: Song of Solomon is published via Amazon.

As soon as this book was published, many have downloaded this book from Academia site – PTL! Here are some places: Lagos, Nigeria; Saha-gu, South Korea; Fuller Theological Seminary; Brisbane, Australia (Oikos Church member); Dourados, Brazil; Tama, Japan; Hanoi, Vietnam; Phnom Penh, Cambodia (Read); Anaheim, United States; Irvine, United States (Fuller graduate student); Fort Lee, United States; Shimorenjaku, Japan! I am so happy I can make these commentaries free of charge through Academia.edu. PTL!

4/24: Phnom Penh Bible School decided to use Pastor Pang's book as their freshmen's required reading. PTL! So we printed 100 more copies at Phnom Penh.

PHNOM PENH BIBLE SCHOOL

History: The signing of the Paris Peace Agreement on 23rd October 1991 opened the doors of Cambodia to the world after years of internal turmoil. Opportunities for spreading the Gospel abounded and many congregations were formed or regrouped from remnants of the pre-1975 faithful.

To meet the growing pastoral needs of the Church in Cambodia, Phnom Penh Bible School was founded by the late Daniel Yee-Wah Lam with support from many Cambodian believers and Christian organisations. After negotiation with the Cambodian government, PPBS was officially recognized by the government on 16th March 1992.

PPBS now offers a two year Associate Degree in Christian Ministry (ADCM), and a four year Bachelor in Christian Ministry (BCM) and Bachelor of Theology (BTh). PPBS also offers a Master of Arts in Christian Ministry (MACM). Today there are hundreds PPBS graduates who are serving God around Cambodia.

PPBS is faithfully supported by many churches and Christians from numerous countries. Its main supporting organisation is Country Network (CN), a non profit, non-denominational organisation that was begun by Daniel Lam.

4/30: Catalyst Sunday service. Here is sermon outline!

Title: Showdown with the prophets of Baal
Text: 1 Kings 18:36-40

YOUTUBE.COM
Fire From Heaven! Catalyst Sunday Service 4.30.2023
Join us as Pastor Robert Oh continues our series on Elijah and Standing Strong with a mess...

36 And it came to pass, at the time of the offering of the evening sacrifice, that Elijah the prophet came near and said, "LORD God of Abraham, Isaac, and Israel, let it be known this day that You are God in Israel and I am Your servant, and that I have done all these things at Your word. Hear me, O LORD, hear me, that this people may know that You are the LORD God, and that You have turned their hearts back to You again." 38 Then the fire of the LORD fell and consumed the burnt sacrifice, and the wood and the stones and the dust, and it licked up the water that was in the trench. 39 Now when all the people saw it, they fell on their faces; and they said, "The LORD, He is God! The LORD, He is God!" 40And Elijah said to them, "Seize the prophets of Baal! Do not let one of them escape!" So they seized them; and Elijah brought them down to the Brook Kishon and executed them there.

• FIRE without the altar will cause wild fire!

- God can win the battle alone, but He wants your participation! Repair your altar!
- God will answer our prayer by FIRE!

Three things fell:
1. Fire of the Lord 'fell'
2. People 'fell' on their faces
3. Heads of prophets of Baal 'fell' on the ground.

- Fire of the Lord 'fell' – but until 'Sacrifice' was at that altar, 'FIRE' of the Lord did NOT fall.
    - o Q: What 'sacrifice' do we need to put at our 'altar'?
    - o A: Comfort, Future, Finance, 'Whatever worked before', friends, family...

- When 'Fire' falls, everything at the altar will 'burn'
- When 'Fire' falls down at the altar.. People 'fell' on their faces; Then & only then...
- Heads of prophets of Baal 'fell' on the ground.
    - o Q: But are you ready to decapitate the heads of the enemy when 'Fire' falls down?
    - o Q: Are you a solider fighting the battle or a spectator at the arena, watching the fight?

4/30: Tanaka Strawberry Farm at Irvine. We visited Tanaka Strawberry Farm as a church outing.

STRAWBERRY PICKING TOUR INFORMATION

●Strawberry Picking Season runs thru May!●

Tanaka Farms is famous for our delicious, sweet, and juicy strawberries! Take a wagon ride around the farm. Learn about the farming methods and history of our farm from your friendly tour guide. You will see how fruits and vegetables grow! Make one stop to pick a seasonal vegetable*, and then the last stop on this tour is in the strawberry patch where you can pick and eat strawberries! Everyone will take home a one-pound basket of strawberries! After the tour, visit the Barnyard Educational Exhibit where you can meet and interact with our barnyard friends.

Tanaka Farm History:

Tanaka Farms began with Great-Grandfather Takeo, who was an Issei - first generation Japanese American - who immigrated from Hiroshima-ken, Japan in the early 1900s. After making the arduous journey to California, in 1922, his son, Farmer Grandpa George, who is a Nisei - second generation Japanese American- was born in Dinuba, California. His parents worked on a small farm as farm hands.

Robert Oh
15h · 👥

Tanaka Farm: Fresh Strawberry picking with Catalyst Church family! April 30, 2023.

In 1941 Farmer Grandpa George gets his own truck to ship produce in La Habra, California. But, in 1942 Farmer Grandpa George flees to Utah so he doesn't have to go into the WW2 Internment camps. While in Utah he meets his soon to be wife Grandma Chris! In 1945, after the end of World War 2, Grandpa George and Grandma Chris come back to Orange County and reside in Fountain Valley, where they farmed various properties with tomatoes, vegetables, and strawberries.

In 1957 Farmer Tanaka was born in Fountain Valley. Farmer Tanaka is a Sansei, a third generation Japanese American. From 1977 to the 1990s Farmer Tanaka grows wholesale tomatoes and strawberries. He even gets up to 300 acres and also starts his own packing and distribution across the country! Farmer Tanaka went to Cal State Pomona where he studied Agricultural Business. It was here that he met his soon to be wife, Shirley, as she was studying Nutrition. Shirley also grew up in a farming family in Riverside and is a Sansei.

Like father, like son! Farmer Tanaka and his wife Shirley had their son, Kenny, in 1983...by the time he started preschool in 1986, the agritourism business model was about to become a reality! Bringing Kenny's preschool class out to the farm for an educational tour was the spark! Kids learned about farming, how seeds turn into plants, picked some vegetables, and, of course, picked their own pumpkin! Now, over 30 years later, thousands of school children visit the farm every year!

Most of Orange County, especially Irvine, was farmland until the mid-1950's when tract housing began to take over the cities. Suburban areas began to take over and very few farms have survived this change. Tanaka Farms is the only remaining family-run farm in Irvine that hosts educational and U-Pick tours. The 30 acres on which the farm is currently located, used to be part of a 100 acre strawberry farm.

100

My April Schedule page as an art form: This may become a collector's item 100 years later!

May

5/2: GBC Radio Interview – Two interviews in one day!

KGBN (1190 kHz) is a Korean Christian brokered time AM radio station licensed to Anaheim, California. It serves Orange County and Greater Los Angeles. Rev. Young Sun Lee serves as the president of the Korean Gospel Broadcasting Network, which owns the station. KGBN is one of four radio stations in the Los Angeles area that broadcast entirely in Korean. The others are 1230 KYPA, 1540 KMPC and 1650 KFOX in Torrance, although they have mostly secular formats.

KGBN broadcasts with 20,000 watts by day. But to protect other stations from interference on AM 1190, power is reduced at night to 1,300 watts. It uses a directional antenna at all times. The transmitter is near the Orange Freeway (California State Route 57) in Brea, California.

The station signed on May 18, 1959 as KEZY, an easy listening station known as "K-Easy". However, during construction and prior to its on-air debut, it was legally known by the call letters KDOG. The first voice heard over the 1,000-watt signal was that of K-9 TV star Lassie. Lassie's owner, Rudd Weatherwax, was an investor in both the station and the Disneyland Hotel where its studios were located.

2000's: The KXMX call sign was derived from KXMX-FM, originally 95.9 KEZY-FM. When that outlet became Contemporary Christian music station KFSH The Fish in 2001, the call letters were reassigned to 1190 AM.

2010's: In August 2010 the station was sold to the Korean Gospel Broadcasting Network, which switched the format to Korean-language Christian radio programming. On March 29, 2011, KXMX changed its call letters to KGBN. From the early 1990s I was working with GBC, PTL!

5/2: GBS Fundraising Radio Interview with Pastor John Park.
I called into GBS annual fundraising public event and had an interview. I am always amazed at God's timing when I simply obey; things happen! PTL!

5/3: GMI EM leadership lunch.
Great food & fellowship with GMI EM leadership! We are preparing a revival meeting coming up in May. Let the anointing of Holy Spirit God to pour down upon the church in Jesus Name. Amen!!

5/3: OCMS USA Board meeting via Zoom.
I became Vice-President of OCMS USA Board after 14 years of service. Now I am appointed to represent the group at OCMS 40th anniversary meeting in June. God is so good!

5/5: Catalyst Small Group - Visiting another group.
We have Bob the drummer at Catalyst Church. Jenny and I were honored to be part of his group and shared our mission work in Cambodia.

5/7: Eppipodo Church Sunday Service
I love this church. I ministered at this church several times a year and share what God did in the month of Feb. this year.

5/8-11: Korean Baptist English Ministers Fellowship retreat. It was so much fun to be with other Baptist pastors sharing our lives together.

5/9: Soren Kierkegaard Research Center in Korea began, and I

became its first director. I joined in via Zoom at 3:30AM USA time! Thanks to technology we have today, I was able to share my heart with board members in

Korea about what God is doing in my life and how God wants to use this organization in the future.

한국 키르케고르 연구소
KOREA KIERKEGAARD RC
Robert Oh Pastor
Head of Research Center
+82-44-863-1404
oikosbishop@mac.com
402 20 Shicheongdaero
Sejong Korea

I did not have an ID card for many years, but now I have one! PTL!

5/14: Mother's Day celebration

Robert Oh
May 14 at 10:35 AM
Happy Mother's Day! Jenny got her breakfast in bed today! Thanks kids!

5/16: Trip to St. Olaf College is set with God's favour. PTL!
I made a plan to visit Atlanta and that determined my trip to St. Olaf College. But God already had a plan for me to attend Soren Kierkegaard Seminar hosted by them and invited a professor form Kierkegaard Research Center of Copenhagen as its speaker!

When God puts all these seemingly independent parts as a puzzle, a big picture merge. PTL!

5/16: REAL SELF – How to live as a missionary in LA post Covid-19 is published today.

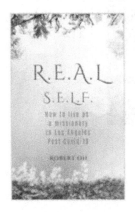

R.E.A.L. S.E.L.F.: How to live as a Missionary in Los Angeles post Covid-19
Kindle Edition

by Robert Oh (Author)   Format: Kindle Edition

See all formats and edi

Kindle
$5.35
You Earn: 27 pts

Read with Our Free App

Introduction for 'To Live as Korean American – Post Covid-19 Pandemic' is the following:

The covid-19 pandemic changed everything - Especially my preaching and teachin schedule! From the end of March 2020 to the end of April, I had to cancel 15 meet

5/16: J & J fellowship at the Source Mall. J.P. said I will be doing this, so I am posting it - and writing it as an entry for Pillar of Fire & Cloud 2023. ☺ So good to share about what our Lord Jesus can do through ordinary people like us. Hallelujah!

5/17: I received this prayer from Vision Church of NY today.
PRAYING FOR CAMBODIA: Moon and Jung Ah's recent missions trip brings our prayer focus to Cambodia today. Cambodia is a country striving to rise from its scarred past. For the first time in many years, Cambodians are experiencing some measure of peace

and freedom. The trauma from Pol Pot's Khmer Rouge regime (1975-1979), its mass evacuation of cities and towns, and the ruthless genocide of those they viewed as opposition can be seen across all generations. One result is that approximately one-half of the population is under 21 and uneducated. Foreign aid accounts for one half of the central government budget. Since the 15th century, Buddhism has been the national religion in Cambodia. Today 85 percent of the population is Buddhist, while less than two percent is Evangelical Christian. In spite of past governmental attempts to eliminate all religions, Christianity has survived. Christians have worshiped openly since 1990, and indigenous church planters have established many new churches. The overwhelming social and emotional traumas of the past have left people open to the gospel. Mature Christian leadership is crucial to mobilize the churches to meet the needs of the people today. (Adapted from Prayercast)

Father, You love Cambodia. We pray for justice and healing spiritually, emotionally and physically from the Khmer Rouge genocide of the late 1970's. We pray for a display of Your power and continued growth within the Cambodian Church. We pray that you would continue to raise up young leaders and messengers to carry your gospel hope into the many villages and cities in Cambodia. Bless and strengthen the many church plants and planters.

In Jesus Name, Amen.

5/19-21: GMI EM Revival meeting

I ministered to Gen. Alpha this weekend. They are those born after 2010! It was so wonderful to connect with GMI young people since my first GMI revival took place 37 years ago.

I am so honored to be able to minister to the next generation of Korean Americans! PTL! God is so good!

5/23: Lunch with Pastor Barry and Dale.

I fond out that Dale's father was an English teacher at Gardena High School, and he was my adviser for Korean Cultural Club I began there in the year 1978. Below is a photo of Mr. Kim on the right and my Dad on the left, as we celebrated 'Partents' Appreciation Night' at Gardena High. We live in a very small world!

5/23: GBS Radio – Hawaii Interview.

When GBS Radio found out that I just published a book on 'Church Planting Case Study of Cambodia' they wanted an interview. It was so wonderful to be able to share what God is doing in Cambodia!

Church Planting Case Study of Cambodia:
2023 Kindle Edition

by Robert Oh (Author), Keo Nang (Author), Pin Ratha (Author), & 4 more   Format: Edition

See all formats and

Kindle
$5.35
You Earn: 27 pts

Read with Our Free App

I taught a ThM class at Cambodia Presbyterian Theological Institute (CPTI) from Febr – April 11, 2023. This book results from six students (Photo above) who shared their stories as Christians and pastors, ministering in Cambodia as church planters. I want thank them for their sincerity and courage in sharing their life so the next generation Cambodian pastors can learn from their experience.

I want to thank all the lecturers and CPTI for letting me use their facility and allowing me to publish this es

My niece from Hawaii sent this photo of her daughter and brightened my day! She is SOOOOOOOOOO cute! Looks just like her Grandmom, my sister, but much whiter!

We will plan to visit her in Hawaii in December this year. By then, she will be 10 months old. I can not wait until I go and give here thousand kisses!

5/28: Catalyst Sunday service - Preaching!

5/30: Lunch with Kevin. So good to connect with wonderful friend!

Robert Oh
Just now ·

Kevin just began his company, and we celebrated God's goodness in his life. He was single at Oikos Community Church many decades ago, now the CEO of his company - how cool is that? PTL!

5/31: Day of Reflection. Thank you, Jesus, for May 2023!

My May Schedule page as an art form: This may become a collector's item 100 years later!

June

6/1: Soren Kierkegaard Research Center of Korea was in the news.

What began as wishful thinking is becoming a reality. PTL!

Our Kierkegaard Research Center in Korea is being recognized by the Christian community of Korea. Our first board meeting was shared at Baptist News of Korea.

6/2: Jenny and I enjoyed our Monday – official rest and date day.

El Dorado Nature Trail, Long Beach: June 2, 2023 (Fri). 6 Minutes Video.
#ElDoradoNature #Trail Welcome to Dr. Bob Oh TV Channel. Thank you so much for your pr...

These are the young people and Pastor Steve who came to Cambodia few months ago. I requested an interview with them so I can learn from frsh eyes about Cambodia they encountered. We met at this hip Mexican Vegan taco and burger joint.

Owner of 'Chicana Vegan' – Jasmine wrote: Chicana Vegana was founded on compassion and love for quality food. As a Mexican-American I loved all food inspired by growing up around the California coast. What I never knew was that I can still enjoy all of these great dishes without the cruelty and with all the taste. I went vegan and created Chicana Vegana to share the amazing food I could recreate. Now my entire familia is vegan! Its been an amazing journey changing our lives and inspiring others to do the same! We found in our personal lives, the ability to embrace a cruelty-free diet while also consuming amazingly delicious food. Well, now we want to share our tasty discoveries with our community while sharing the idea that you never have to compromise compassion and taste. Serving the community doesn't just come on a plate. We aim to support local community groups such as outreach groups, animal sanctuaries and educational institutions through event fundraising. Chicana Vegana seeks to build lasting and flourishing relation

6/5: Eighth book of the year and #87th book of my life just got published! Thrilled!

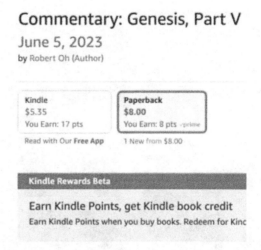

Commentary: Genesis, Part V

June 5, 2023

by Robert Oh (Author)

Kindle	Paperback
$5.35	$8.00
You Earn: 17 pts	You Earn: 8 pts ✓prime
Read with Our **Free App**	1 New from $8.00

Kindle Rewards Beta

Earn Kindle Points, get Kindle book credit
Earn Kindle Points when you buy books. Redeem for Kinc

6/6: Ninth book of the year and #88th book of my life just got published! Thrilled!

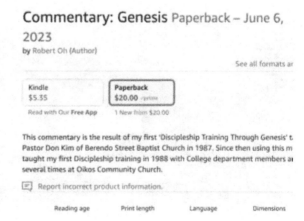

Commentary: Genesis Paperback – June 6, 2023

by Robert Oh (Author)

See all formats ar

Kindle	Paperback
$5.35	$20.00 ✓prime
Read with Our **Free App**	1 New from $20.00

This commentary is the result of my first 'Discipleship Training Through Genesis' t.
Pastor Don Kim of Berendo Street Baptist Church in 1987. Since then using this m
taught my first Discipleship training in 1988 with College department members a
several times at Oikos Community Church.

Report incorrect product information.

Reading age	Print length	Language	Dimensions

When I combined all five commentaries of Genesis, a total of 1200 pages were produced. Since KDP Amazon's publishing limit is 825, I had to cut out 400 pages. I think cutting out the process was much more difficult than adding 400 pages. But it is done, and now I have a book that can 'stand on its own.'!! PTL

6/7: Nine years ago today!

I love it when FaceBook reminds me of what happened so many years ago today. Nine years ago today, I was in Seattle with Jenny celebrating Bophal's wedding. Since we met her in 2007, Jenny and I have treated her like our younger sister, and it moved us to see her happy with Brian. First time walking down the aisle with a bride as her guardian.

Thank you Jesus for such a privileged life Jenny and I have in Christ.

6/8: Loyalty is a sign of Royalty!

Loyalty is a sign of Royalty! Are you a child of King of Kings and Lord of Lords? Then be 'loyal' to those your King allowed to have in your life! We met in our 30's and now entered our 60's together for His Kingdom! These two brothers from the Valley Methodist Church have been faithful supporters and intercessors for my ministry from Oikos Church era to Cambodia mission. Thank you brothers!

6/9: Genesis Lab Devotion meeting. I rode Jack to Orange Country this morning to share what God is doing in Cambodia. Thank God for the partnership and friendship we have in Christ.

6/9: Soren Kierkegaard Research Center Korea zoom meeting with Prof. Jon Stewart.

Thank God for Zoom! Kierkegaard Research Center leadership had a zoom meeting with Dr. Jon Stewart, before publishing his book in Korean. He is now officially our partner in crime and wrote a wonderful preface to his book.

Preface to Korean translation: 《쇠렌 키르케고르 입문 : 주관성, 아이러니, 현대성의 위기》 trans. by Changwoo Lee and Jeong In Choi, SeJong: Karis Academy 2023.

It is a great pleasure for me to see my book now appear in the Korean language. I hope that it will help Korean readers appreciate the thought of Denmark's most famous thinker, Søren Kierkegaard. Although Kierkegaard lived in the nineteenth century in a quite distant culture, I believe he still has something important and relevant to say to all of us today.

The book is an introductory text intended to present Kierkegaard's life and thought to interested readers. In writing this work I wanted to show how Kierkegaard was inspired by the ancient Greek philosopher Socrates and how he used him as a model for his own thinking. Kierkegaard discusses Socrates at length in one of his first works, *The Concept of Irony*, from 1841. From this point onward, until his death in 1855, he continued to use Socrates as his main point of orientation for his own writings. Like Socrates, Kierkegaard did not claim to know anything or to teach anything to others. Instead, his goal was to raise important issues about, for example, life, death, faith, God, marriage, love, despair, and doubt. Then through his writings he tried to get his readers to think about these issues for themselves. Just as Socrates saw himself as a gadfly, provoking his fellow Athenians to thought and reflection, so also Kierkegaard tried to be the gadfly of Copenhagen.

One of his most important ideas concerns the absolute and irreducible value of each individual human being. In our busy and confused modern times, it is easy to be overwhelmed by the sense of how small and apparently insignificant we are as individuals in the vast globalized world or indeed in the infinity of the universe itself. But Kierkegaard believes that each of us has the ability of find meaning in our own existence. He recognizes that there are no easy solutions in such matters, and that uncertainty and anxiety are a natural part of the human condition. However, he helps us to become aware of who we are so that we can continue as individuals while still fully recognizing the challenges that we face as existing human beings. His mission is not that of a dry scholar who is interested in convincing his readers of some abstract truth by means of step-by-step discursive arguments. Instead, like Socrates, he tries to lead his readers to find the truth within themselves. His focus is not on academic argumentation but rather on living.

I hope that Korean readers will find the value of Kierkegaard's approach in their own lives, as they confront the struggles of existence that Kierkegaard knew so well. I am very grateful to Changwoo Lee and Jeong In Choi for their translation and for their engaged work, together with Robert Oh, to introduce Kierkegaard in

Korea. I am delighted to contribute in my own small way to their efforts. – Jon Stewart.

6/11: Have you tried Samin from Hawaii?

The best 'Samin' I had in my life is not at Hawaii, but at Gardena Bowling Café. Since I had morning off before going to The Well Church, I decided to make a visit. I was not disappointed!

6/11: Visiting The Well Church

After the service, as I was walking out with Pastor James of the Well Church, an older gentleman greeted me by my name. What a surprise! He said that we met 20 years ago when he was an elder of a church where I led a revival meeting. He is now a pastor of the Korean Church that hosts English speaking 'the Well Church.' What a small world! We will meet when I get back from Europe tour in July. Thank you Jesus for your supernatural connection!

6/12: Prof. Jun joins teaching Ruth in Cambodia.

I am writing a commentary on the book of Ruth after finishing the commentary on Genesis.

Prof. Jun graciously agreed to teach on this book of the Bible to selected Cambodian pastors.

They will be teaching and preaching out of it and combined their efforts with my commentary and eventually publish them in English and Khmer.

6/12: Missionary Kim of Jesus Village Cambodia visits us!

Wonderful crab dinner and fantastic fellowship! Oh what a night!

6/12: Our first zucchini of the year!

Jenny loves to pick vegetables and fruits from our backyard.

We planted zucchini as soon as we arrived in USA in April. We are already seeing the fruit of our labor and increase water bill. ☺

6/13-16: St. Olaf College – The Hong Kierkegaard Library visit.

Thank God we finally met and had wonderful meeting. I shared about our Kierkegaard Research Center in Korea via Power Point over the lunch and was appointed as an international board member representing Korea – PTL! Anna is the new director of the center and her husband is a professor and a life long friend to Jon Stewart. Once again, what a small world we live in. I found some information on them at their webpage: Anna and her husband Brian: Brian's areas of specialization are Philosophy of Religion, Existentialism, and the thought of Søren Kierkegaard. Brian has a Ph.D. from the University of Copenhagen, a master's degree from Yale University, and a bachelor's degree from Utah State University. He is the author of The Isolated Self: Truth and Untruth in Kierkegaard's On the Concept of Irony as well as numerous articles and book chapters. He was part of the team that translated

Kierkegaard's Journals and Notebooks (11 volumes) and has served as co-editor of Kierkegaard Studies: Yearbook and Kierkegaardiana.

6/14: Dinner at my adopted spiritual brother David's house with his favorite wife!

David's Mom, Esther Mom (that's how I addressed her) adopted me as her 10th child. She and Pastor Sam Choe had 9 children together. But at Dominican Republic mission conference she wanted me to become her 10th child.

They live about 45 minutes away from St. Olaf College, so I made a visit and shared from heart to heart about honoring our Dad in assisting in 'finishing well.' We will have a meeting in July at Seattle for that with Pastor Sam.

6/16-19: Atlanta, GA - Pastor Ree's Church visit.

When we planted our 5th Oikos Church in LA, he was an original member. I think we had around 10 people in our first gathering.

Then he went to Siberia with me and almost died! Long story! But that made him to reflect on his own life and planted the Jesus Street Church in Korea.

FaceBook sent this photo that 10 years ago today Jenny and I met him and his wife at the Jesus Street Church of Korea. We look so young then! ☺

I ministered to his people at Atlanta Methodist Church English ministry team. God moved so wonderfully! PTL!

6/20: Father's Day celebration – One day later.

Robert Oh

Celebrating belated Happy Father's Day dinner with the family! This lobster gave his life so we can have a feast!

Since I was in Atlanta on Father's Day, our kids decided to take me out for lunch the next day.

We went to a nice Chinese restaurant for a lobster noodle dish – and this 4 lbs lobster was the only one they had. Sorry Charlie!

He died for us so we can enjoy a wonderful $120 lobster noodle dish! ☺

6/21: Wonderful lunch with Pastor Ken of Ttk Kamsa Church.

I think his middle name is 'faithful.' He has been such a faithful friend for more than 30 years. The church moved back to Korea Town so we decided to celebrate. We had 'Gamja-tang' together. It was the best 'Gamja-tang' in my life.

What is it? Gamja-tang or pork back-bone stew is a spicy Korean soup made from the spine or neck bones of a pig. It often contains potatoes, cellophane noodles, dried radish greens, perilla leaves, green onions, hot peppers and ground sesame seeds. The vertebrae are usually separated with bits of meat clinging to them. The name "gamjatang" is a play on words. Gamja means potatoes, but the dish isn't named after this tuber. The name refers to the pork-spine bone which is also called gamja. It is this bone that adds the flavor to the broth.

6/22: Dr Sung of California Baptist University.

Robert Oh
1d · 🌐

Having wonderful fellowship with Dr. Sung at CBU and meeting his staff at the office of student success! God is good!

What a glorious ride to Riverside on Jack! I love to ride my motorcycle on crisp sunny morning of Southern California.

I met Dr. Sung when he was a college student. He met me in his dreams for many years and got connected at a revival meeting and once more at 40 days fasting and eventually worked at Oikos Church as a staff.

He now leads a large office of student success, supervising over 10 directors of the university programs. I had such a wonderful time sharing our Lord Jesus Christ and what He can do through our lives. God si so good!!

6/22: Oasis House Report. Great report from Cambodia! Oasis House conducted a wonderful staff care day – PTL!

6/22-24: JC Bridge Retreat at Orange Country.

I was so happy to see 14 young people who graduated from High School and ready to enter college.

We spent three days together sharing from our hearts what it means to have Real Self Identiy in Christ.

We worshipped together and spent much time praying and playing together. Thank you Jesus!

6/20: Daniel's Face Book Entry – on Time Management, Burnout.

I just read this interesting book (Four Thousand Weeks) that's ostensibly about time management but is really a philosophy about spending time. It includes this story (possibly apocryphal) attributed to Warren Buffett, where he's asked how to set personal priorities and I've been thinking about it for days.

Buffett allegedly says to make a list of the top 25 things you want out of life and arrange them in order, from most important to least. The top 5 are the ones around which you should organize your time. But contrary to expectation, the remaining 20 aren't the ones you should get to when you have the opportunity. Instead, they're the ones you should *actively avoid at all costs*. These end up being goals that aren't important enough to form the core of your life, but they're seductive enough to distract from the things that matter most. Man, I've been thinking about that a lot. I think there's truth to it, and it relates to the basic thesis of the book: there is not enough time to do everything, so we need to be intentional about what we don't do, not just what we do. It's easy to try to eliminate things that seem like an obvious waste of time (although the book questions this premise a bit also - being "productive" frequently means pushing out the life you want to live to the future, and some things that in a production-based society seem wasteful are actually what life is about, being fully in the present). But what's really required is eliminating things that are ostensibly good, in favor of things that are better or more personally important.

Kind of coincidentally, I read this book right after reading another fascinating book - The Burnout Society by Byung-Chul Han. I can never recall where I get book recs so I have no idea how I found out about either, and reading them back to back was not intentional, but they share a bit of a common theme. The Burnout Society is curious because the author is South-Korean born and educated, but he's a philosopher who lives and teaches in Germany. That's a unique story. Anyway, it's a philosophy tract written in German and it reads like it - dense and difficult language. But it has some interesting ideas.

The main question it considers is why modern society is so depressed and burnt out. His thesis is that it reflects a shift in society itself, from a negative society (based on rules of what you should and should not do) to a positive society (you can do anything you want). The pathology of a negative society is things like neuroses and criminality, the pressure of societal expectation. But in a positive society, what drives us is internal - if we can do anything, there's a sense that we must do as much with ourselves as we can. And this internal drive to maximize what we do leads to depression (when our lives don't measure up to what it seems it should be) and burnout (when we can't keep up).

I have some quibbles with the book but I do think there's insight in that idea. At the very least, if you think about it, burnout is a really odd phenomenon. It's not like everyone who's being burnt out is forced to work that hard. Perhaps superficially their job requirements seem that way. But there are other job options. And as both books point out, it's frequently the most successful and wealthy that drive themselves the most, are most susceptible to burnout. It has to be that something is driving us internally. Which is weird. As Han writes repeatedly, we have become our own oppressors.

127

The combined advice would seem to be that if you feel overwhelmed, recognize that it's largely based on unreasonable internal expectations so adjust those. If you can't do everything (and you can't) then logically you must fail to do some things so choose what to fail at or ignore intentionally and chill out.

To this entry, I wrote to him on the FaceBook wall:

Robert Oh
thanks for this post. so helpful. i just bought both books.. i will do book talk on them later. may i share your post with others? we need to talk abt this.. very much in line with Soren Kierkegaard's teaching.

6/25-27: Copenhagen, Denmark - Soren Kierkegaard Research Center visit.

Robert Oh
1d · 🔾   ...

덴마크 키르케고르 연구소 방문 리포트: 6월 27일 2023년 (화요일). 9분 비디오.

YOUTUBE.COM
덴마크 키르케고르 연구소 방문 리포트: 6월 27일 2023년 (화요일). 9분 비디오.
닥터 밥오 TV 방문을 환영 합니다. 구독 좋아요 그리고 종싸인을 같이 중보기도와 함께 눌러 주시면 감사하겠...

It was so wonderful to have our Soren Kierkegaard Korean books to be part of Copenhagen Soren Kierkegaard Research Centre. Dr. Garff and I had a wonderful discussion about how we can work together to bring the message of Soren Kierkegaard to the next generation of Christians.

128

6/27-30: Oxford, UK - OCMS 40th Anniversary Celebration.

It was so good to see old friends and academic mentors at OCMS on our 40th Anniversary celebration!

6/28: Now I am on Podcasts!! All 3000 postings!

I met lots of people challenging me to turn my YouTube teaching content to Podcasts, but did not know how. I learned from Dr. YouTube how to do it in 4 minutes this morning and was able to convert all of my content as Podcasts within one hour. I love this era we live in.

I don't complain about the danger of technology but use it to expand the Kingdom of God in Jesus Name. Amen!!

6/29: My riding buddy Mike is taking another crazy long solo ride to Alaska. The title of his article in Korea Times reads, 'From Venture to Adventure!' Praying for safe travel.

My June Schedule page as an art form: This may become a
collector's item 100 years later!

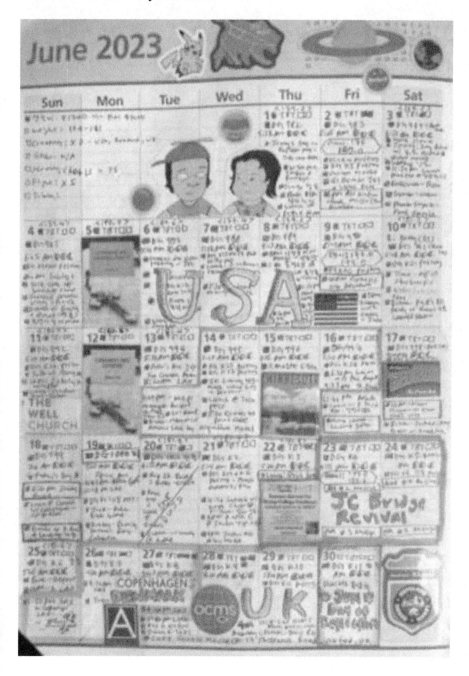

131

July

7/1: London - Les Miserable at Sondheim Theatre.

My friend Sypho of Cambodia asked on my FaceBook entry of this photo: What is 'Les Miserable, Pastor?' So here is the response from the Web world: Les Misérables, colloquially known as Les Mis or Les Miz is a sung-through musical with music by Claude-Michel Schönberg, lyrics by Alain Boublil and Jean-Marc Natel, and a book by Schönberg and Boublil, based on the 1862 novel of the same name by Victor Hugo.

The original French musical premiered in Paris in 1980 with direction by Robert Hossein. Its English-language adaptation by

producer Cameron Mackintosh with lyrics by Herbert Kretzmer has been running in London since October 1985, making it the longest-running musical in the West End and the second longest-running musical in the world after the original Off-Broadway run of The Fantasticks.

Set in early 19th-century France, Les Misérables is the story of Jean Valjean, a French peasant, and his desire for redemption, released in 1815 after serving nineteen years in jail for stealing a loaf of bread for his sister's starving child. Valjean decides to break his parole and start his life anew after a bishop inspires him with a tremendous act of mercy. But a police inspector named Javert refuses to let him escape justice and pursues him for most of the play. Along the way, Valjean and a slew of characters are swept into a revolutionary period in France, where a group of young idealists attempts to overthrow the government at a street barricade in Paris.

This is my 19th times watching this musical. To many people, I am insane!

Søren Kierkegaard' Jump:
Don't be afraid to become that Individual!
There is nothing with which every man is so afraid
as getting to know how enormously much he is capable of doing
and becoming that Individual.

Don't expect world to understand you.
The world understand me so poorly that they don't
even understand my complaint about them not understanding me.

7/2: London Wimbledon Korea Church Sunday Service

런던윔블던한인교회
Wimbledon & District
Korean Baptist Church

It was wonderful opportunity to meet with Pastor Enoch Kwon of Wimbledon Baptist Church and his wife again.

She gave her life to serve God full time during one of my college revival meetings few decades ago at New Jersey and I had privilege of minister to her church from Nottingham, London and now at Wimbledon, UK. God is amazing God, but lives of His children together like a puzzle – PTL!

Lead Pastor J Kwon wrties: I hope God's abounding grace will be with everyone who visit us, the Wimbledon Korean Church.

On the first Sunday of December 1999, pastor Doohyeong Ha held the first worship service at Merton Park Baptist Church in London with God's guidance. Afterwards, in 2015, we started worshipping at the current venue, St. James Church.

Over twenty years, all members have been praying for and pursuing the one goal: "a God-pleasing church." On top of this goal, we will keep on becoming "Church-like church." We all are building this church as a true church, the body of the Lord, in order to please God's will.

I hope you meet Jesus Christ, who has expressed the perfect love on the cross, and you become God's joy.
7/4: Pastor Gordon of Oxford's Email – Sharing his poem!

Gordon & Rachel Hickson

Gordon Hickson wrote:
Wow! You are busy, and remarkably productive! I'm amazed at the volume of material you are creating. I enjoyed listening to some of your podcasts and heard you talking of post Covid19. You may enjoy this poem which God downloaded to me on Pentecost morning 2020 as we settled into lockdown. It was like a trumpet call for the church not to miss this opportunity. Back in September 2019 I sat down and began writing a book on Kingdom leadership called " The Heavenly Virus!" I had no idea what was about to break globally!

135

Søren Kierkegaard wrote, "Who is a poet? He is an unhappy man who conceals profound anguish in his heart. Yet whose lips are so formed that as sighs and cries pass over them... they sound like beautiful music." I hear that profound anguish from Pastor Gordon in his poem.

Here it is:

THE "HEAVENLY VIRUS": GOD'S RESPONSE TO COVID 19!

IN 2020 COVID VIRUS HIT THE NATIONS OF THE WORLD
BUT STRANGELY THIS WAS ALSO WHEN GOD'S GLOBAL PLAN UNFURLED

RAISING LEADERS IN THE CHURCH WHO SAW WITH PERFECT VISION TO IMPART FAITH AND HOPE AND RECONCILE DIVISION

THESE WERE THE DAYS OF LOCKDOWN WHICH STOPPED US IN OUR TRACKS WHEN OUR OLD WINESKINS FAILED, REVEALING ALL THE CRACKS

WE SAW SO CLEARLY THEN THAT IT'S "NOT BY MIGHT OR POWER" "BUT BY GOD'S HOLY SPIRIT" WHO IS NEEDED IN THIS HOUR

AS IN THOSE DAYS OF OLD - THERE IN JERUSALEM
WITH THOSE DISCIPLES LOCKED DOWN, IN THAT UPPER ROOM
IT SEEMED TO ALL THE WORLD THAT DAY THAT ROME HAD CLEARLY WON

BUT LITTLE DID THEY KNOW RIGHT THEN, THAT GOD HAD JUST BEGUN!

AS THOSE NAILS PIERCED HIS HANDS, AND THAT SPEAR PIERCED HIS SIDE
THE WORLD GREW DARK AND GREY, EVERY HOPE AND DREAM JUST DIED

THERE ON THAT CROSS AT CALVARY, THE DEVILS FURY WAS OUTPOURED

BUT GOD REACHED DOWN AND SEIZED THAT CROSS, AND IT
BECAME HIS SWORD!

THERE IT WAS THAT GOD HIMSELF, MADE A SPECTACLE AND
STRIPPED

THE DEVIL OF HIS POWER AND SAW ALL HIS DEMONS WHIPPED!
THAT MOMENT COULD HAVE EASILY BROUGHT A GLOBAL WIDE
DISASTER

BUT HERE IS WHERE OUR LORD BECAME OUR KING AND SOVEREIGN
MASTER

SO TODAY WHEN IT JUST SEEMS THIS VIRUS MIGHT HAVE WON
WE ALL NOW NEED TO COME TO FAITH THAT OUR GOD HAS JUST
BEGUN!

OLD WAYS, TRADITIONS, WINESKINS, – ALL OF THESE HAVE
STOPPED

AND GOD HAS PRUNED HIS CHURCH, AND ALL RELIGION HAS BEEN
CROPPED

NOW IT IS OUR GOD'S TURN – TO SEND HIS "HEAVENLY VIRUS!"
A GLOBAL WIDE AWAKENING, A REVIVAL FLOW AMONGST US
GONE ARE ALL THE MAN-MADE HEIRARCHIES AND STRUCTURES
THINGS THAT MADE US STERILE, WITH FEAR, CONTROL AND
RUPTURES

THIS IS THE DAY WE NEED TO SEIZE, GOD'S CHURCH MUST BE A
"MOVEMENT"

EVERY BELIEVER NOW EMPOWERED TO KNOW WE'RE "HEAVEN-
SENT"

DISCIPLED BY SERVANT LEADERS WHO KNOW HOW TO EQUIP
AN ARMY OF BELIEVERS – EACH ONE HELD "IN HIS GRIP!"

LIKE THOSE LEPERS IN LOCKDOWN, BACK IN ELISHA'S DAY
WE ALL WILL SOON DISCOVER THAT THE ENEMY MUST PAY!

EVERY CRIPPLING CONSTRICTION, EVERY LIMIT NOW HAS GONE
OUR ENEMIES HAVE FLED AWAY, IN TERROR AND ABANDON

NOW WE'RE WALKING OUT, TO A TOTALLY NEW LANDSCAPE
MILLIONS ONCE CAPTIVE, ARE SEEKING ALL WAYS TO ESCAPE
THESE MONTHS OF THIS CRUEL VIRUS SHOWED THE PEOPLE THEY
CAN'T COPE

NOW THEY'RE YEARNING DEEP INSIDE FOR OUR MESSAGES OF
HOPE. GOD HAS SHAKEN, AND HE'S SHAKEN – JUST HIS REALM NOW
REMAINS

GONE ARE THE EXCUSES, THE DECEPTIONS AND THE GAMES
PEOPLE ARE JUST CRYING FOR RELATIONSHIP AND TOUCH
GOD'S SIGNAL TO US ALL, WHO'VE BEEN GIVEN SO SO MUCH!

SO COME ON ALL YOU LEADERS, LET'S ARISE AND LET US SHINE
LET'S MAKE GOD'S LOVE GO VIRAL! COME ON! NOW IT'S OUR TIME!
LET'S RISE UP WITH HIS WEAPONS OF UNITY AND PRAYER

LET'S DEMONSTRATE WITH GRACE TO ALL - THAT WE CARE AND
YES, WE DARE!

7/3: Copenhagen, Denmark – Again!
I had to come back to Denmark to save several hundred dollars!

Direct flight from London to Los Angeles increased my airfare by at least $400. Well, I had no choice. Jesus saves, so I have to save!

I had to make a stopover at Copenhagen again in order to save on airfare. But it turned out to be a blessing, because I was able to meet Dr. Ole of OCMS. He was my PhD cohort; we suffered together! We talked about our future work in Nepal together. God willing, we will be in Nepal together.

Sharing a quick 'Crispy Chicken Burger' at Central Train Station in Copenhagen, Denmark with Dr. Ole and his favorite wife! We suffered together through PhD research stage at OCMS, UK! Suffering brings people together! 😃

7/4: Back to USA on Fourth of July

It's so good to be back home after 10 days of traveling! We had Fourth of July Celebration with Ribeye steaks and picked vegetables from our backyard. God is so good!!

Independence Day, known colloquially as the Fourth of July, is a federal holiday in the United States commemorating the Declaration of Independence, which was ratified by the Second Continental Congress on July 4, 1776, establishing the United States of America. But for most Americans, it's just a wonderful BBQ day!

7/5: Orange County Cannan Mission Sending off Service

I was so happy to see these young people being sent away to Mexico as a part of a short term mission. The best way to taste what it means to live missionally is to go on a mission trip and experience it personally!

7/6: We found a Cambodian restaurant in my city.

According to one study, there are about 320,000 Cambodian Americans in the United States. California has the highest population of Cambodian Americans with an estimate of 118,000 people. Long Beach, California has the largest and oldest Cambodian community in the nation with at least 20,000 people. I was told that there are 65,000 Cambodians in Long Beach before but I was told wrong!

Which US state has the most Cambodian population? Based on Wikipedia Demographics, these are the result: The states with the highest concentration of Cambodian American residents are Rhode Island (0.5%; 5,176), Massachusetts (0.4%; 25,387), Washington (0.3%; 19,101), California (0.2%; 86,244), and Minnesota (0.2%; 7,850).

7/8: I designed this book cover for Lee Yong Un.

Classics: Winner of the 4th Chung W. Bae Literary Award Prize Paperback – July 8, 2023

by Yong Un Lee (Author), Michelle Chung (Editor)

See all formats and editions

Kindle	Paperback
$3.50 after credits	$7.50
You Earn: 15 pts	You Earn: 8 pts
$5.00 before credits	1 New from $7.50
Read with Our Free App	

'When You Are in Los Angeles' by Yong Un Lee has been selected as the 4th winner of the Chung W. Bae Literary Award, which was established to honor literary achievement of the late Poet Chung W. Bae who left a huge mark on Korean-American poets society. Chung W. Bae Literary Award is organized by 'Miju Poetry and Poetics' (publisher, Michelle Chung), which, founded by the late Chung W. Bae in 2004, has been publishing top-notch poems by American as well as Korean-American poets.

This is my third book cover design for Chung W. Bae Literary Award Prize publication. I met Michelle Chung at Eppipodo Church several years ago, and we have been working together to making Korean poets to publish in English in America. Mr. Lee writes:

The Sound of Shower I heard
Under the Rusty Tin Roof

Here in Los Angeles, rain is never enough and we worry about drought every year. We expect less than enough rain this year again but it rains hard today. It makes me feel good to see the dark cloud filled up to the end of the sea.

The news I was named the winner of the Chung W. Bae Literary Award was the sound of blessed rain falling on the dry wilderness. No, for me it is more like the sound of shower I heard under the rusty tin roof. I am sure the persimmon tree in my house will produce more leaves after this rain.

I am so happy to be the winner of this great award. I would like to give thanks to publisher Michelle Chung and Poet Kyungla Ahn for letting me have the opportunity to turn in my poetry works in 『Miju Poetry & Poetics』 to be published. I am also grateful to the judges for selecting the poem of a novice poet. ~ Yong Un Lee

Classics*

Starlight, a beauty's wink knocks on the window the moment I turn on the button she is already here, lovely Genie, with sharp long fingernails Arabian nights where people buy and sell dreams in a blue smoke seductive jungle black leopard's yellow eyes are meowing at night the magician Genie's uvula gets wet tenderly Persian princess Genie's sensually puffy white chest is dreaming at Eros' door quietly ajar there white bright full moon Genie takes her clothes off like snow falling in a cotton field as time scintillatingly soaks

Ah –
I would run to be there.

*The title from the poet Oh Jang-Hwan's eponymous poem

7/8: Catalyst Church Big God small group at our house

As they would say in England, "They are such lovely people!"

Jenny and I had a blast hosting them at our house for the second time. We made Korean Kalbee BBQ and they brought feast fit for a kings and queens! We ate like there is no tomorrow and feasted on sharing out testimonies – God is so good!

7/9: Catalyst Church Sunday Service.

Pastor Robert continues our series on Facing Giants with a sermon encouraging us to stand against our false self and allow our destined self to shine through.

When I preach at Catalyst church, I would say, "There are two kinds of people in the world!" And they made a T-Shirt stating that and honored me with it before my preaching session. So out of about 8 billion people in the world, there are two kinds of people – Those cool people who have this

T-Shirt and those who wish they could own such a 'to-be-a-collector's-item' in the distance future! ☺

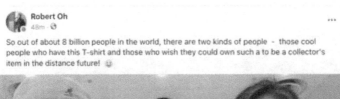

So out of about 8 billion people in the world, there are two kinds of people - those cool people who have this T-shirt and those who wish they could own such a to be a collector's item in the distance future! ☺

7/10: Dr. Bob Oh TV – YouTube Channel.

Dr Bob Oh TV

I think it took more than 2 years to have 1,000 subscribers for my YouTube Channel. I am thankful that I can reach more people with the Daily Gospel and Book Talk.

1,000

Subscribers

Covid-19 literally took away my traveling engagements away but God gave a different means to reach lot more people from all over the world! PTL!

7/11: Martin Buber said, "All Life is Encounter!"
Well, that happened today! Praise the Lord!

As I joined an effort to launch a Kierkegaard Research Center in Korea, I am meeting wonderful scholars and professors who have been studying Søren Kierkegaard! So fun to talk about our mutual hero and learn from each other!

7/12: 'Love your Mac!' missionary to Japan!

James and his wife served at Oikos Church for many years before they went to Japan as a missionary few years ago.

So good to hear what God is doing all over the world with His servants brining the Gospel to everyone from everywhere!

7/13: Commentary on Ruth published.
I was able to publish this commentary before leaving to Cambodia! PTL! I used Pastor Pang's Korean commentary for this volume. So THANKFUL!!

Commentary: Ruth Paperback – July 13, 2023
by Robert Oh (Author)

See all formats and e

Kindle	Paperback
$3.85 after credits	$8.00
You Earn: 17 pts	You Earn: 8 pts
$5.35 before credits	1 New from $8.00
Read with Our **Free App**	

Report incorrect product information.

Reading age	Print length	Language	Dimensions
12 - 18 years	129 pages	English	6 x 0.33 x 9 inches

7/13: Martin Buber said, "All Life is Encounter!," Part II.
Well, that happened today - **again**! Praise the Lord - **again**!

On June 11th entry of this book, I shared how I met these two brothers at Gardena – The Well Church.

We decide to actually meet and share our life together. It turned out that we have so many mutual friends. We live in a very very small world! Such a real kindred spirits! We will be working together in the near future! PTL!

Below is June 11th Entry:

6/11: Visiting The Well Church

After the service, as I was walking out with Pastor James of the Well Church, an older gentleman greeted me by my name. What a surprise! He said that we met 20 years ago when he was an elder of a church where I led a revival meeting. He is now a pastor of the Korean Church that hosts English speaking 'the Well Church.' What a small world! We will meet when I get back from Europe tour in July. Thank you Jesus for your supernatural connection!

7/14: Drinking Coffee with Kierkegaard is published.

This is my second attempt to publish a book on coffee and bring Søren Kierkegaard's philosophy into it. I logged in 500 coffee-tasting results here!

I wrote in my introduction of this book the following:

This little book on coffee is a result of my travel to 64 countries and drinking coffee there. At one point, I started to rate my experience in numbers. Giving 10 maximum points on three categories: Flavour, Fragrance, and Force (Intensity). As of this writing, I have tasted more than 600 coffee, but I have decided to publish my first book limited to the first 500.

7/15-17: Seattle Hyungjae Church.

Pastor Kwon Joon of Hyungjae Church invited me to speak at all three service. We met in 1991at LA event hosting Pastor Ha Yongjo of Ohn Nu Rhe Church of Korea.

Since then he came to Seattle 24 years ago and built this church. I would have to say this was one of the healthiest church I visited in America! PTL! I had such wonderful time ministering to both Korean speaking and English speaking congregations! PTL!

Several thousand members of the church worked

together like one body of Christ! Wow!

After the second service, a grandmom approached me and said, "I taught you at the Yong Dung Po Church Kindergarten under Pastor Pang Jiyil!" How is it possible? I met my teacher, who taught me 55 years ago. She is in the middle of three teachers! Teacher Shin!

7/20: Daily Gospel - The completion of Genesis!
On Daily Gospel Day # 1031, I finished my teaching / sharing on Genesis! I am so thankful!

Daily Gospel 1031: The death of Joseph! Gen...
#Genesis, #BibleStudy, #QT #BibleCommentary
Amazon link: https://tinyurl.com/3b22n3sa...

매일 복음 1031일: 요셉의 죽음! 창세기 50:22-26. ...
#창세기, #성경공부, #매일복음, #하나님말씀, #복음,
#QT, #큐티 #신학 #공부법 #꿀팁 닥터 밥오 TV 방문...

7/22: Korea - Kierkegaard Research Center conference
Pastor Lee Changwoo and I first met in April 2022. We felt we need to work together. We put everything we desired into action. Within 15 months, we published several books together, held several meetings together, started a center together and

now hosting our very first Søren Kierkegaard Conference at our center at Sejeong City! If this isn't God, how can we explain this?

We had almost 50 people show up to this event and celebrate together what God is doing in our lives through the teaching of Søren Kierkegaard. I felt such a kindred spirit with these wonderful people – Hallelujah! Thank you Jesus!

Let me trace back how it all began on March 21, 2022:

March 21, 2022 (Monday): Third Study Begins…

Today's Reflection: Today is the last day. I am so thankful that it is over by today. I had a hiccup in my 21 days fasting this time! I meant literally! Seven days of non-stop 3 second interval hiccup really challenged my mind, body and spirit. God broke through and had an incredible encounter with God, along with Jenny on my side as it happened. PTL! The Third Study began for me.

A revised and modified entry from my diary: *'I don't want to study about Kierkegaard - I want to be Kierkegaard'* is the main theme of my writing at Soren Kierkegaard Center, Copenhagen, Denmark. Writing a post-doctorate poetry based play as a final project dealing with existential salvation enhancing concept of evangelical view on Grace using Gap & Eul understanding between God and us.

Most likely I will be traveling to Denmark often now and report back to my readers with new adventure and new books on following the Holy Spirit God.

April 25-26, 2022: Jenny back to USA and Robert is visiting Saejeon city and meeting Pastor Lee – One who is crazy about Kierkegaard.

We became instant best friends! Pastor Lee is really a genuine existentialist and Kierkegaardian at heart. We talked for hours and I invited his entire family for a dinner at the fanciest restaurant of Sejong City. He already published many volumes of Kierkegaard's work into

Korean. I have a feeling we will be working together very closely in the future. PTL! This is one of the highlight of my visit to Korea!

July 19, 2022: Pastor Lee Changwoo of Korea posted this on his Face Book wall in Korean and it is Google Translated (& edited):

I'm giving you the news.

Tumblbug funding has been completed for [Learn from Birds and Lilies]. This time, with the help of missionary Robert Oh many people who participated in funding abroad.

Thanks to those who personally supported me, those who regularly sponsored me, those who participated in the Tumblbug funding approximately 7.8 million won ($ 7,000) was raised to publish the book.

This time [Learn from Birds and Lilies] will be published in Kierkegaard series published in 1847, and will be published in three volume books. If possible, we will finish final edits this week so that the books will be available in the second week of August.

Planning for the future: Part 1 is being prepared for publication with Rev. Yoon Deok-young, who is in charge of Samsung Church in Paju, and part 3 is being prepared with Missionary Robert Oh. In the future, we ask for your prayers and support so that we can publish quality books quicker and more efficiently.

Aug. 26, 2022: Korea trip - I arrived at Korea and took KTX train to Sejoeong City and had wonderful fellowship with Pastor Lee's couple and Pastor Park. I ended up ministering at River of Nation Church for their Friday night service. Wow.

Sep. 3, 2022: Soren Kierkegaard Research Centre launch.

  Pastor Lee Changwoo of Karis Academy published this book and honoured me as a co-writer. I am so glad God made our path cross in April this year. He did a special lecture on Søren Kierkegaard and I was so blessed by depth of his understanding on Søren's philosophy and its practical implication for today's context.

Oct. 29, 2022: Donated my book to Orange County Korean Community Center book cafe! My Jack accompanied me there. It is a beautiful day to ride in L A. PTL!

I donated my book on Søren Kierkegaard to Orange County Korean Community Center. Since I was attending Julie's book publication celebration there I befriended a man in charge of Book Café of that facility and donated my book there. God is so good! He requested that I hold a seminar for community center members in Saturdays!

Nov. 29, 2022: Our Karis Academy books from Korea on Soren

Kierkegaard made it to the bookshelf of St. Olaf Kierkegaard Library – PTL!

I was so thrilled to receive this photo from Soren Kierkegaard library of St. Olaf University. Pastor Lee Changwoo woked so hard for these volumes for last 10 years. Finally, they are shared at St. Olaf Kierkegaard Library – PTL!

Feb. 11-13, 2023: Kierkegaard Retreat with Suwon Hana Church.

When Pastor Koh contacted me about leading this revival retreat he asked me to preach minimum 90 minutes per session four times! What kind of request is that? But once I met more than thousand participants from 7 Hana Baptist Churches all over Korea I understood 'why' such request was made. They were so hungry for God and His Words – I ended up teaching 100 minutes per session. At the end of two days, Pastor Koh invited those who want to give their life as a full time ministers or missionaries, more than 100 came forward and received prayer. It was truly a revival time! Thank you Jesus!

Feb. 17-18, 2023: Revival meeting at Joyful Church with Pastor Cho Jihoon.

 I held three different meetings for this church

Then we had Karis Academy's Book Publication celebration meeting with Pastor Lee Changwoo.

Pastor Lee Changwoo did a superb job of informing and inspiring all the participants to read Soren Kierkegaard more seriously and apply his teaching into our lives. I was so happy to be there and learn from the master!

June 1, 2023: Soren Kierkegaard Research Center of Korea was in the news.
What began as wishful thinking is becoming a reality. PTL!
Our Kierkegaard Research Center in Korea is being recognized by the Christian community of Korea. Our first board meeting was shared at Baptist News of Korea.

June 9, 2023: Soren Kierkegaard Research Center Korea zoom meeting with Prof. Jon Stewart.

Thank God for Zoom! Kierkegaard Research Center leadership had a zoom meeting with Dr. Jon Stewart, before publishing his book in Korean. He is now officially our partner in crime and wrote a wonderful preface to his book.

Preface to Korean translation: 《쇠 렌 키르케고르 입문 : 주관성, 아이러니, 현대성의 위기》 trans. by Changwoo Lee and Jeong In Choi, SeJong: Karis Academy 2023.

It is a great pleasure for me to see my book now appear in the Korean language. I hope that it will help Korean readers appreciate the thought of Denmark's most famous thinker, Søren Kierkegaard. Although Kierkegaard lived in the nineteenth century in a quite distant culture, I believe he still has something important and relevant to say to all of us today.

The book is an introductory text intended to present Kierkegaard's life and thought to interested readers. In writing this work I wanted to show how Kierkegaard was inspired by the ancient Greek philosopher Socrates and how he used him as a model for his own

155

thinking. Kierkegaard discusses Socrates at length in one of his first works, *The Concept of Irony*, from 1841. From this point onward, until his death in 1855, he continued to use Socrates as his main point of orientation for his own writings. Like Socrates, Kierkegaard did not claim to know anything or to teach anything to others. Instead, his goal was to raise important issues about, for example, life, death, faith, God, marriage, love, despair, and doubt. Then through his writings he tried to get his readers to think about these issues for themselves. Just as Socrates saw himself as a gadfly, provoking his fellow Athenians to thought and reflection, so also Kierkegaard tried to be the gadfly of Copenhagen.

One of his most important ideas concerns the absolute and irreducible value of each individual human being. In our busy and confused modern times, it is easy to be overwhelmed by the sense of how small and apparently insignificant we are as individuals in the vast globalized world or indeed in the infinity of the universe itself. But Kierkegaard believes that each of us has the ability of find meaning in our own existence. He recognizes that there are no easy solutions in such matters, and that uncertainty and anxiety are a natural part of the human condition. However, he helps us to become aware of who we are so that we can continue as individuals while still fully recognizing the challenges that we face as existing human beings. His mission is not that of a dry scholar who is interested in convincing his readers of some abstract truth by means of step-by-step discursive arguments. Instead, like Socrates, he tries to lead his readers to find the truth within themselves. His focus is not on academic argumentation but rather on living.

I hope that Korean readers will find the value of Kierkegaard's approach in their own lives, as they confront the struggles of existence that Kierkegaard knew so well. I am very grateful to Changwoo Lee and Jeong In Choi for their translation and for their engaged work, together with Robert Oh, to introduce Kierkegaard in Korea. I am delighted to contribute in my own small way to their efforts. – Jon Stewart.

June 13-16, 2023: St. Olaf College – The Hong Kierkegaard Library visit.

Thank God we finally met and had wonderful meeting. I shared about our Kierkegaard Research Center in Korea via Power Point over the lunch and was appointed as an international board member representing Korea – PTL! Anna is the new director of the center and her husband is a professor and a life long friend to Jon Stewart. Once again, what a small world we live in. I found some information on them at their webpage: Anna and her husband Brian: Brian's areas of specialization are Philosophy of Religion, Existentialism, and the thought of Søren Kierkegaard. Brian has a Ph.D. from the University of Copenhagen, a master's degree from Yale University, and a bachelor's degree from Utah State University. He is the author of The Isolated Self: Truth and Untruth in Kierkegaard's On the Concept of Irony as well as numerous articles and book chapters. He was part of the team that translated Kierkegaard's Journals and Notebooks (11 volumes) and has served as co-editor of Kierkegaard Studies: Yearbook and Kierkegaardiana.

June 25-27, 2023: Copenhagen, Denmark - Soren Kierkegaard Research Center visit.

It was so wonderful to have our Soren Kierkegaard Korean books to be part of Copenhagen Soren Kierkegaard Research Centre. Dr. Garff and I had a wonderful discussion about how we can work together to bring the message of Soren Kierkegaard to the next generation of Christians.

I am still amazed at the speed in which Korean Kierkegaard Research Center came about – PTL!!

Robert Oh
1d

덴마크 키르케고르 연구소 방문 리포트: 6월 27일 2023년 (화요일). 9분 비디오.

YOUTUBE.COM
덴마크 키르케고르 연구소 방문 리포트: 6월 27일 2023년 (화요일). 9분 비디오.
닥터 밥오 TV 방문을 환영 합니다.구독 좋아요 그리고 종씨안을 같이 중보기도와 함께 눌러 주시면 감사하겠...

7/23: Pastor Sunny at Christian International Church

Pastor Sunny of Christian International Church gave testimony before I preached that he met God and dedicated his life to serving God at the JAMA conference in the USA in 2000.

I was amazed by God's grace and demonstration of His power – what one message from the Lord can do to people! PTL!

7/23: One Day Revival at Karis Church of Sejeong

Pastor Lee Changwoo holds a Sunday service at Søren Kierkegaard Research Center and I was invited to hold its very first One Day Revival at his Karis Church! I was honored and pleased to share my life with him and his congregation.

카리스 교회 1일 부흥회 | 오석환 선교사 | 2023년 7월 23일

7/24-25: Back to Cambodia
Wow. This is my fifth country to visit in July. I passed out during the flight and woke up when they made the announcement that we are landing at Phnom Penh Airport. At the airport our faithful Daroth was waiting for me to take me to home away from home – Arata Oasis House. PTL!

7/26: Hun Sen hands over power to Manet.
This is a very important news from Cambodia. I wanted to make sure I put this information in my book.

In a landmark announcement that marks the end of an era in Cambodian politics, long-serving Prime Minister Hun Sen has confirmed that he will not retain his position in the next government. Instead, his son Hun Manet will succeed him, a seismic change set to occur in the coming weeks. This revelation came during a special audio address to the nation on the afternoon of July 26. Hun Sen's surprising decision was revealed subsequent to a meeting with King Norodom Sihamoni.

"My son is not inheriting this role without a legitimate process," Hun Sen reassured the nation. "He has participated in the election as a lawmaker candidate, a fundamental step in our democratic system. Looking to his own future, the outgoing prime minister sketched out his post-leadership plans. "I will maintain my presidency of the ruling party and remain a member of parliament," he noted. "Furthermore, upon my departure from the Cabinet, the King has offered to appoint me as head of the Royal Advisory Council," he added.

Hun Sen is also slated to fill the shoes of the retiring Senate President Say Chhum. However, he emphasised the importance of respecting the boundaries of power in his new role. "Although I will replace Senate President Say Chhum, it's crucial to understand that I will not intrude into the responsibilities of the new prime minister," he declared. This commitment underscores a distinct separation of power, hinting at a potentially new political dynamic in the coming era of Cambodian politics.

Memo: Our work in Cambodia will be determined by how political climate change – So we need to be in prayer mode to adjust and move where God is leading us!

7/25-29: Arise Asia! at Bangkok, Thailand.

From 25-29 July 2023 in Thailand, the Arise Asia gathering will bring together students and young leaders across Asia and the Middle East who are passionate about their Christian faith and intent on learning more about missions and what God is doing around the world.

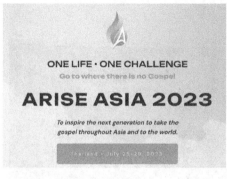

During the gathering, younger leaders between the ages of 18-30 will be inspired by the Great Commission, hear fresh ideas for missions, and take the next step to go where there currently is no gospel. There will also be incredible ways to interact with others who are passionate about their faith in God.

Participants can expect to learn from experienced global missions practitioners from across Asia, with plenty of opportunities to ask questions from speakers, plus evening cafés to connect with each other. The program will maximise participant engagement through innovative lab sessions. Seminars will address critical missions issues in the world, including how to prepare to go into missions, internship opportunities, the persecuted church, discipleship, spiritual and mental health, church planting, unreached people groups, international development, business as mission, justice issues, and more.

Arise Asia is co-hosted by: Asia Evangelical Alliance, Asia Theological Alliance, Asian Access, CCCOWE, Evangelical Fellowship of Thailand, Lausanne Movement in Asia and Movement Day.

My FaceBook friend reported on his wall: It's all about God and His glory. 1,800 from 37 countries came before the Lord for repentance and surrendering. Around 300 actually responded to go out for 1-2 year of missionary works overseas.

My friends from New York and New Jersey were there to head up the prayer team. So good to see them.

I led one workshop on 'Hearing God's Voice.'
I made a QR Code for the video at YouTube.

7/28: A poem for the day!

Our Real Work
It may be that when we no longer know what to do
we have come to our real work,
and that when we no longer know which way to go
we have come to our real journey.
The mind that is not baffled is not employed.
The impeded stream is the one that sings.

Wendell Erdman Berry: He is an American novelist, poet, essayist, environmental activist, cultural critic, and farmer. Closely identified with rural Kentucky, Berry developed many of his agrarian themes in the early essays of The Gift of Good Land and The Unsettling of America. Wikipedia

Born: August 5, 1934 (age 88 years), Henry County, Kentucky, United States.

7/29: Back to Cambodia
So good to see my favorite wife again. She suffered through a major cold/flu for the last 10 days! Poor thing! Pray that Lord will completely heal her in Jesus Name. Amen!

7/30: 6AM - A Revelation at the pool.

I was doing my regular one hour swim from 6AM – 7AM, God spoke to me about turing the month of July diary into a book entitled, 'Living Like Kierkegaard: July 2023.' WOW! Thank you Lord! There were few more major revelations that will require for me to travel... I will share that when things get settled. God is good!

7/30: Worship Service at Encounter House

So good to be back at home in Cambodia and attend our Encounter House Church at Arata Residence. PTL!

7/31: Living Like Kierkegaard: July 2023 is published! PTL!

Look inside ↓

Living Like Kierkegaard: July 2023 Paperback – July 31, 2023

by Robert Oh (Author)

See all formats and e

Kindle	Paperback
$3.85 after credits	$8.00
You Earn: 17 pts	You Earn: 8 pts
$5.35 before credits	1 New from $8.00
Read with Our Free App	

I want to 'live' like Søren Kierkegaard. I met too many people wanting to talk about existential philo but refusing to live as an existentialist! Most likely, Søren Kierkegaard would not want to be identifi an existentialist, but he did start a philosophical movement called 'existentialism.' Maybe we can jus copy and try to live like Søren Kierkegaard as just a Kierkegaardian!

I composed a poem, pearling Søren Kierkegaard's thoughts in one place. What I did in July 2023 can

My July Schedule page as an art form: This may become a collector's item 100 years later!

August

8/1: Day of Reflection for July & celebration for #10,000 written prayer.

TALK WITH GOD no breath is lost.
WALK WITH GOD no strength is lost.
WAIT WITH GOD no time is lost.
TRUST IN GOD you will never be lost.

27 years ago, I started numbering my prayer in my diary. Today I wrote my prayer #10,000. As I reflect on the last 27 years, I realize all the prayers I have written, nothing is lost.

God answered so many of my prayers I can just write a testimony book on that. Thank you, Jesus!

8/2: Oasis House Wednesday morning Devotion
I shared my July with Oasis House staff. I challenged them to 'Jump' and obey God when He speaks to them.

8/3: Bob's 44th spiritual birthday
I turned 44 years old today – spiritually. Aug. 3, 1979 – 9:30 PM, Jesus became REAL to me! PTL! My life in Him continues now in Cambodia.

8/4: Lunch with College buddies.

We met each other at UC Berkeley campus in 1979! That's 44 years ago. Four of us are now living in Cambodia. One is a retired dentist who became a missionary to Cambodia. The other is a businessman who lived here for several years now. The other is my friend since Junior High School – that makes our friendship lasting more than 50 years! Only God can put all of us at Phnom Penh Carl's Jr. Hamburger joint today! PTL!

8/4: Hosting a missionary couple for dinner at Oasis House.

 I met this ex-missionary to China couple at Seattle last month. Now they are in Cambodia leading a short term team from Hyung Jae Church. They are will come back to Cambodia as full time missionary in September. I am so amazed at how God puts together a wonderful

8/6: Encounter House Sunday Service - Sermon on PHO!

 I shared a message on PHO – Pray, Hear and Obey! Since we had young people who only spoke Khmer, I had to share a very simple message.

8/8: Brown Café – Guess whom I met at Brown Café of Aeon Mall.

 I ran into Oasis House volunteer staff at Brown Café at Aeon Mall II. What a pleasant surprise. Since the current metro area population of Phnom Penh in 2023 is 2.3 million people, meeting them at a café is like winning a Lotto! We shared our love for Christ Jesus and coffee – in that order! ☺ They asked me to pray for them, and I prayed for them sincerely.

8/8: August Swimming Log.

I want to qualify for Iron Man – at least in the swimming portion. That means I have to swim 2.4 miles (3.86 km) non-stop! I swim about 60 minutes – 90 minutes each morning. But most Ironman events have a time limit of 16 or 17 hours to complete the race, course dependent, with the race typically starting at 7:00am. The mandatory cut off time to complete the 2.4-mile (3.86 km) swim is 2 hours 20 minutes. The mandatory bike cut off time for when an athlete must have completed their swim, transition and bike varies generally between 10 hours and 10 hours 30 minutes from when an athlete began their swim. The mandatory run cut off varies between 16 and 17 hours from when athlete began their swim. That means I have to finish my swim within 2 hours and 20 minutes! Can I do it?

8/9: CPTI graduation

Cambodia Presbyterian Theological Institute (CPTI) celebrated its' 20th-year graduation! 65 students graduated, and so many friends and family came it was standing room only celebration – PTL! Two of my ThM students graduated last year, and one is now working as a lecturer at CPTI. God is so good! The following is their mission statement: 1. CPTI trains pastors and missionary who can serve the Presbyterian Churches in Cambodia; 2. CPTI seeks to train national and global leaders contributing to the society and nation in the areas of the NGOs, Christian schools, business, social welfare

168

organizations, and civilian services, etc.; 3. CPTI emphasizes the cultural mandate of Christians in which every Christian should become a light and salt of the society and nation.

8/10: Søren Kierkegaard book we published in Korea was chosen by World Korean Christian Media Association for its reading competition.

8/12: Breakfast fellowship with Pastor Noah and his favorite wife.

Pastor Noah is a professional singer turned missionary to Cambodia. He asked me to be part of his 'Healing Concert' last year and I had so much fun reading my poetry and singing my song at this Mini-Concert at 'Blessed Bean Café.' He and his wife joined us at Oasis House. Since she is a certified art therapist, she enjoyed walking through Oasis House counseling rooms.

8/13-27: Jenny's trip to Chiang Mai.

Jenny and Oasis House staff went to Chiang Mai, Thailand, for their two weeks of training! Jenny suffered from nasty cold and flu for more than two weeks and we weren't sure if she can make it to this trip, but by God's grace she got well enough to travel this time with her beloved team sisters! That means I would have to be all alone again for two weeks! I was planning to to travel to Philippines, Brunai and Vietnam – but toward the end, I felt compelled to just stay home and wrap up many things that I need to finish.

8/13: Children of Light Church – Sunday service.

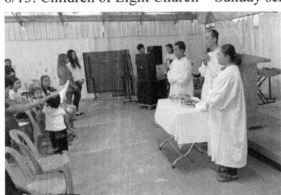

I love this church! Every time I have a chance to minister here, I make time to do it. I get blessed to witness authentic discipleship taking place in Cambodia. Missionary Ji was able to build a community of followers of Christ within his church. PTL! They are taking part in the Lord's Supper!

8/15: Lunch with Joseph Hwa and his fiancée.

I met Joseph at GMI of Fullerton, USA. Pastor Steve Kang introduced him as a potential missionary to Cambodia and so we got connected and we did several YouTube open mentoring sessions together on topic of how to prepare to become a missionary to Cambodia. Two years later, he is now a missionary in Cambodia and will be married to this beautiful Khmer lady in December this year, serving a local church plant in Cambodia. God is so good!

8/15: CRRC 10th year celebration Zoom meeting.

Ten years ago today four brothers got together and launched Cambodia Research and Resource Center (CRRC). We were so young then! Even the kids in the photo are all grown up, one of them even got married! How time flies!

8/15: I just swam my first 2.7 miles today!

On the August 8th entry I wrote: "I want to qualify for Iron Man – at least in the swimming portion," and I accomplished it today! PTL! That means I have to swim 2.4 miles (3.86 km) non-stop! Since the mandatory cut-off time to complete the 2.4-mile (3.86 km) swim is 2 hours 20 minutes, I have to swim within that pace. Today I swam 2.7 miles in 2 hours and 20 minutes, a bit more than required!

8/16: Visiting Phnom Penh Bible School.

YOUTUBE.COM
Phnom Penh Bible School (프놈펜 성경 학교): Aug 16, 2023. (1:25 video)

8/18: Missionary Kim will be using Pastor Pang's book to train 60 Cambodian pastors!

We met almost 20 years ago at the missionary training program hosted by GMI in Korea. He and his wife were so committed to Cambodia but were discouraged by leadership who did not want them to go to Cambodia but go where there weren't many Korean missionaries! I did the total opposite – I asked him, "Did God tell you to go to Cambodia?" He said YES, and so I told him to come to Cambodia even if there are 20,000 Korean missionaries in Cambodia! Well, they are here and discipling many Khmer pastors now – PTL!

8/20: Jenny's book 'Living Tree, Dead Branches' is ready to be published in Korea. !

Sarah Lee of Oasis House translated Jenny's English book to Korean. Initially we wanted Kyu Jang Publishing House to publish it in Korea, but it seemed God had a different plan. Karis Publishing House, which publishes all of Søren Kierkegaard's book took the challenge. I pray that this book will be read by multitude who need to hear how God still heals today

8/22: Qualifying for Ironman swim three times!

Since I swam and qualified for Ironman swim on August 15th, I was able to duplicate the record two more times! Now I need to ride my bicycle 112 miles and run full marathon after the swim! ☺

This is the history of the Ironman competition: The single-day endurance event now known as IRONMAN was the brainchild of Judy and John Collins, a couple who moved from California to Hawai'i in 1975. The Collins family participated in the Mission Bay Triathlon in San Diego on 25 September 1974. That event now marks the start of modern triathlon in the U.S.

In 1977, the Collins' involvement in organizing a sprint run-swim competition in Honolulu helped plant the seed of an idea to put on a triathlon event the following year. Their goal was to create something for the endurance athletes—those who favored events such as the Waikiki Roughwater Swim and the Honolulu Marathon over short sprint events. But where would the bike leg be? The answer came to them early in 1977, when John thought of using a local bicycling club route. Judy and John said to each other, "If you do it, I'll do it," and John famously added "...whoever finishes first we'll call him the Iron Man."

At the Waikiki Swim Club banquet in October, 1977, Judy and John announced their Around the Island Triathlon, to take place the following year. When John described the three triathlon legs, the swimmers laughed. The couple's dream was that many would enjoy swimming, bicycling and running non-stop for 140.6 miles. They dreamed that their triathlon would become an annual event in Hawai'i. On February 18, 1978, Judy and John Collins saw their dream come true with the first-ever Hawaiian Iron Man Triathlon. Little did they know then what a phenomenon their race would become, and how many lives it would impact.

8/22: Hun Manet, Hun Sen's son, officially becomes the prime minister of Cambodia today.

From the Phnom Penh Post: Hun Manet is now officially the Prime Minister of Cambodia after the National Assembly (NA) gave him a vote of confidence on the morning of August 22, the second day of the inaugural session of the NA's 7th legislative term. Outgoing NA president Heng Samrin read the outcome of the vote, declaring that 123 of the 125 members of parliament voted in favour of Manet.

The plenary session also gave a vote of confidence to Khuon Sudary, electing her as NA president, the first woman ever to assume this role.

Manet, 45, is the lawmaker for Phnom Penh. He succeeds his father former Prime Minister Hun Sen, who had been in power for nearly four decades. Hun Sen remains president of the ruling Cambodian People's Party (CPP), which won 120 out of the total 125 parliament seats in the July 23 general election.

King Norodom Sihamoni has bestowed upon Manet the horrific "Kitti Tesaphibal Bindit," a title for a leader with profound knowledge and highest intelligence who will lead the country to greater prosperity.

8/23: Jenny's Forever 41 birthday today!
Since she is in Chiang Mai, Thailand – we had to send her love via friends who are traveling with her. Kids called her via FaceTime and I set up a surprise party during lunch time.

8/23: The book on Ruth ends and the Lamentations of Jeremiah begins at Dr. Bob Oh TV.

This commentary on the Lamentations is a result of my Daily Gospel teaching on Dr. Bob Oh TV YouTube Channel: https://tinyurl.com/5knavyrw.

I incorporated Pastor Pang Chi Yil's Korean commentary in the teaching and utilized Pastor Ha Youngjo's notes on daily questions.

According to the Oxford Bibliographies: The book of Lamentations expresses the humiliation, suffering, and despair of Jerusalem and her people following the destruction of the city by the Babylonians in 587 BCE. Traditionally attributed to the authorship of the prophet

175

Jeremiah, Lamentations was more likely written for public rituals commemorating the destruction of the city of Jerusalem and its Temple. Lamentations is notable both for the starkness of its imagery of the devastated city and for its poetic artistry. The book consists of five poems, the first four written as alphabetic acrostics proceeding through the alphabet from *aleph* to *tav*, while the fifth evokes the alphabet with its twenty-two-line structure. While scholars for a time found the primary theological purpose of the book in the Deuteronomic righteousness - reward theology with its hope in the possibility of repentance, more recent discussions have viewed Lamentations as an unresolved expression of grief following the trauma of Jerusalem's devastation. Because of its focus on grief following devastation, Lamentations speaks not only to the specifics of its own historical circumstances, but also to the timeless human experience of life."[3]

8/27: Sunday service at Phnom Penh Thmei Community Church with Pastor Kim! PTL!

I brought Pastor Pang's book 'The Christian Life' as a gift to all the members of the church. 'Why do you believe?' was the theme and the challenge!

---

[3] https://tinyurl.com/4a6w2y4w, accessed on 2 Aug. 2023.

8/27: Jenny and Oasis House staff came back from Chiang Mai, Thailand. It's good to have Oasis House team back!

8/29: Jenny's book is now officially published in Korea and sold through Yes 24 – it's Korean version of Amazon.

We published through Karis Publishing. I pray that many people will read this book and be healed in Jesus Name. Amen!

I will be going to Korea in September and promote this book at many meetings, especially those who wrote recommendations for this book!

8/29: Joel Copple Invitational Meeting - I shared my thoughts on

Gap & Eul to 33 heads of Cambodian Christian agencies since this meeting is officially called, 'The Heads of Agencies Meeting.' ☺ Of course, the photo of the meeting was not allowed to be shared with the public due to security reasons!

8/30: Swimming 2.5 miles (4000 km) every day for ten days!

August 2023

Pool Swim	
4,048M	Today
Pool Swim	
4,048M	Tuesday
Pool Swim	
4,002M	Monday
Pool Swim	
4,025M	Sunday
Pool Swim	
4,070M	Saturday
Pool Swim	
4,002M	Friday
Pool Swim	
4,002M	Thursday
Pool Swim	
4,070M	8/23/23
Pool Swim	
4,025M	8/22/23
Pool Swim	
4,324M	8/15/23

Since I swam and qualified for Ironman swim on August 15th, I was able to duplicate the record a total of 10 times today! And ask I have stated before all I have to now is to train to ride my bicycle 112 miles and then run a full marathon after the bike ride! ☺ Maybe I can use my motorcycle for the competition, then I may be able to finish the race.

When I swam my first 4,324 meters on August 15th, the average time for 100m was 2' 47'' (2 minutes and 47 seconds). But today, after 15 days of training, I was able to lower the average swim time of 100m to 2' 16". That's 31 seconds improvements on every 100m of swim, which is fantastic record! PTL! I swam for one hour and 32 minutes today.

8/30: Jenny's belated birthday celebration at the Pizza Company. Good food, and great fellowship for a great price! I love Cambodia!

8/31: Living Like Kierkegaard: August 2023 is published! PTL!

I want to 'live' like Søren Kierkegaard. I met too many people wanting to talk about existential philosophy but refusing to live as an existentialist! Most likely, Søren Kierkegaard would not want to be identified as an existentialist, but he did start a philosophical movement called 'existentialism.' Maybe we can just try to copy and try to live like Søren Kierkegaard as just a Kierkegaardian!

179

My August Schedule page as an art form: This may become a collector's item 100 years later!

September

9/1: Day of Reflection for August 2023.

Jenny and I have this getaway hotel in Phnom Penh. On my day of reflection, I decided to check in and spend the whole day together. Having a nice dinner at their French restaurant is the highlight of the trip.

9/2: McClaren 720S at Phnom Penh, Cambodia!
I found this super car in front of a furniture store!

Starting at $310,500

Highs Overflowing wow factor, track-capable but street-friendly, zero-to-120 mph in less than seven seconds. Lows Costs like the average US house, subpar brake-pedal feel, you better like attention from strangers.

9/3: Encounter House at Oasis House

Encounter House Community

Encounter House Sunday worship service now meet at Oasis House weekly – PTL!

9/4: Missionary Dongkyu Kim teaching on tithing!

Missionary Dongkyu faithfully teaches 'Tithing' using my book. Many pastors are learning and then bring the book to their churches. Many churches have become self-sustaining by teaching tithing. PTL!

The following is the introduction to this book:

It's not about money – but it's about faith. I was fed up with all the interviews I was doing in Cambodia, Thailand and Vietnam. Many of the Christian leaders and pastors were certain that their churches could not become financially independent because of so many legitimate and logical reasons: we are too poor, we are under communism, we are culturally, socially and politically made that way. As I was researching for my PhD proposal at Oxford Center for Mission Studies (University of Wales, England), all I heard were certainties on how it was impossible for them to become financially independent.

Finally, at my last interview in Vietnam, I met Pastor H. He was a young pastor in his thirties, with fire in his eyes and confidence in his tone of voice. As I opened the interview with the comment, "So, I heard that it is very difficult for Vietnamese churches to become financially independent at this time...," he questioned me back right away, "Who told you that?" "Well, just about everyone I have met so far," I responded. Pastor H told me an entirely different story. For the last five years, he has been planting churches in Vietnam and out of 20 or so churches about 80% of them are already financially independent. "But how?" I asked. To that he smiled and simply pointed to the Bible and said, "What does the Bible say? It tells Christians to tithe." He explained to me that when his new church has more than ten families, one local pastor receives a full salary based on the average economic standard of that village.

I was so surprised to find such a pastor, and I was even more surprised that answer was so simple. "What does the Bible say?" It is not a economical, political, cultural or social issue. But do we really believe the Bible to be the Word of God and are we as

Christians willing to live according to the ways of God mandated in that Book? I realized it was not about money, but it was about our faith in God and His ways.

I pray that this book will change your life.
If you are tithing already, then you will be able to confirm that and will be pleased to know that you are on the right track. If you are not a tither, this book is for you. Are you a Christian? Do you really want to please our Lord Jesus Christ? And do you want to live by the Bible, the Word of God? Then read on, you will become a better follower of Christ at the end of this book.

Tithing is a solution to most of Cambodian Christian churches' financial problems. If every professing Cambodian Christian would tithe, every congregation would be free of financial worries and could begin truly to be "the salt of the earth." Churches would no longer struggle to pay their bills: pastor's salary, electricity, ministry fund, and even mission fund.

9/5: Swimming 4 km (2.5 miles) per day is going great!
The most important number to observe is Avg. Pace. I did 100 meter in 2 minutes and 14 seconds. That is a very good number! For example, my July 30th swimming 1.5 Km was at 3 minutes and 59 seconds per 100 meters. This means I shaved off 1 minute and 55 seconds per 100 meters! That is an awesome improvements!

9/6: Meeting church member in the airplane.

I was flying to Siem Reap to attend Phnom Penh Forum

conference and met Sohmi (One in sunglass) of Encounter House Church. We live in a very small world. I sat next to her co-worker from Bangladesh and shared about our life – she as an NGO worker and me as a missionary!

9/6: Surprise at the Wake Park, Siem Reap!

At International Christian Fellowship of Siem Reap: Meeting old students of El Shaddai Bible School. Wow! I taught them 18 years ago and we lost contact. They saw me at the ICF café and recognized me! How cool is that? You can scan the QR code and see the Wake Park and my friends!

Met my students from El Shadai Bible School of Kampong Cham by accident at Wake Park, Siem Reap! We met in mid 2000 - so almost 20 years ago! Amazing! God is so good!

I met Kelvin at the Wake Park. He and his family moved to Siem Reap, Cambodia from Hong Kong to serve young people of Cambodia. I am so happy to see young people using their talents and gifts to serve the Lord.

The Wake Park was a fantastic place. I would love to come here and enjoy this multi million dollar wake board fun – you are pulled by a cable taking you all around the water park!

9/6: Face Book's Entry – 6 years ago today!

Six year ago today I spent time with my Mom at the hospital. She fell, and we had to take her to ER. This hospital refused to let her go to her apartment until she was fully recovered! She went hunger strike for almost three days! She was so fiercely independent she hated being at the hospital, where her freedom was taken away. I asked my Mom to pray for me for my travel and she did such a heart felt prayer I wept all the time she was praying. Then afterward she gave this beaming smile! I am so glad Face Book sent this photo to me.

9/7: Stephen's 35th birthday.
My phone Siri suggested that I call my son for his birthday! It's a crazy idea that my phone can let me know of such data.

9/7: Kohker Temple, Angkor Wat Tour.

Kohker Temple, Angkor Wat: WOW!! Sep. 7, 2023.

Scan the QR code and you can watch the video!

Cambodia's Koh Ker Temple archaeological site has been officially added to UNESCO's World Heritage List, during the 45th session of the World Heritage Committee held in Riyadh, Saudi Arabia, on September 17.

The Phnom Penh Post

Joy as Koh Ker Temple registered by UNESCO

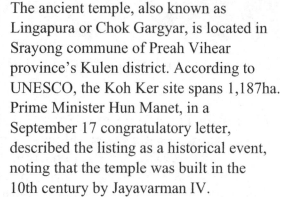

An aerial view of the 10th century Koh Ker Temple complex in Preah Vihear province. UNESCO

The ancient temple, also known as Lingapura or Chok Gargyar, is located in Srayong commune of Preah Vihear province's Kulen district. According to UNESCO, the Koh Ker site spans 1,187ha. Prime Minister Hun Manet, in a September 17 congratulatory letter, described the listing as a historical event, noting that the temple was built in the 10th century by Jayavarman IV.

The temple was accepted to the list by the International Council on Monuments and Sites (ICOMOS) as one of the world's top architecture sites, he added.

9/8: Phnom Penh Forum - Siem Reap Conference.

Missionary Yang and I have been working on Cambodian Proverb book for last 3 years. Yang did an excellent presentation and I followed up with a few comments. Small number of people attended but it was worth a trip to Siem Reap!

9/9: Donating Pastor Pang's book at OMF Cambodia.

Missionary Cho introduced me to a fellow OMF missionary when he was dropping me off at the Siem Reap airport and by God's providence, we sat together at the airplane. I shared about Pastor Pang's book! and she wanted to have them at OMF headquarters library. She also studied philosophy at undergrad, so I gave her my Søren Kierkegaard books.

9/9: Hosting Elder Sam from USA

Elder Sam was my college department student in 1986 at Berendo Baptist Church. He has been faithful disciple of Jesus Christ and made a commitment of 3 years in the mission field. He chose Cambodia as one of the

188

nation he wanted to come. The Southern Baptist Board will do some more interviews and finally make decision but we are hopeful that they will come to Cambodia next year!

9/9: Ministering at Young Intellectual Group of New Life Church

It was wonderful to minister to Young I group of New Life Church again. The church had 50 years celebration of Pastor Taing's golden anniversary and 50 years of service to the Lord. It was a massive celebration at the church and they gave them a brand-new car as a gift.

I have known them since 2007 and they are amazing leaders and faithful servants of the Lord. PTL!

9/10: Going to Siem Reap to see Mike.

I was notified that Mike had a stroke and hospitalized at the local clinic.

I took the next flight to Siem Reap from Phnom Penh, and arrived at the hospital to find Mike going in and out of consciousness. It was unbelievable to to think that I just had him say last Wednesay at his house how he is so happy in his life!

I shared the gospel with him when he was conscious and was able to communicate with me through blinking of eyes or squeezing of hands. I believe he responded positively to my invitation to accept Christ as his personal savior and Lord.

9/11-15: Oasis House - Lay Counsellor Training (LCT) week
First Khmer languate LCT is held at Oasis House this week.

9/12: Dinner with RUPP ex-student!

It is always a special treat to share a meal with formal student who continues to connect and stay relavent to the life topics we discussed at philosophy class at RUPP!

9/13: Brother Bong Café of Siem Reap.

1. Brother Bong Cafe

⊙⊙⊙⊙⊙ 351 reviews · Closed Today
Coffee & Tea, Cafe · $

"A coffee connoisseur's trip to Siem Reap is not complete without a visit to..."
"Delicious breakfast in Siem Reap "

This was #1 Coffee shop of Siem Reap, chosen by Trip Advisory, so I made a visit. Fantastic place!

9/12: Søren Kierkegaard zoom lecture

I was so tired from traveling so I really couldn't stay awake but Pastor Lee had a wonderful lecture on Søren Kierkegaard and Jon Stewart's book on Søren Kierkegaard. We had people from Korea mostly but I joined in from Cambodia and Pastor Choi from USA. I love Zoom!

9/13: Devotion at LCT

I shared my heart at LCT Devotion at Oasis House and they prayed for me and Mike! We prayed for his salvation in Jesus Name. Amen!

9/13: Phnom Penh News of the day

Kampot provincial police have announced measures to contain a recent spike in antisocial behaviour by "unruly" youth. Officials say the province has been plagued by recent violence among so-called "gang members", who often fight with weapons such as knives and machetes. Several social observers have praised the administration's swift actions to restore social order, noting that members of the public have expressed their fears that their frequent brawls could lead to wider violence.

The Kampot police announced that a 2am curfew would be in effect for all suspected gang members from September 7 onwards. The police of the province's nine towns and districts announced plans to mount patrols and round up any suspects believed to be involved in "chaotic activities".

San Chey, executive director of the NGO Affiliated Network for Social Accountability, cautioned that any measures taken by the police should be based on clear principles in order to avoid any accusations of discrimination or injustice. He said nationwide police measures to curb offences more promptly and efficiently may increase the public's trust.

"The police should consider two important factors – gatherings that could lead to gang violence, and the possession of weapons. Of course the police must be quick to respond to either of these scenarios, but it is also critical that the public report any such incidents as soon as they notice them," he added.

9/13: My Korean poems published!

Our 14th Epipodo poetry book will be published in Korea and there will be a publication party in Oct. in Korea. Jenny and I will be in Korea during that time, so we will attend – PTL!

오석환 박사(Sukhwan Robert Oh, California, Cambodia)

오석환(시인, 선교동원가, 교수)은 미국 버클리대 철학과, 풀러신학대학원 석사, 목회학 박사, 영국 옥스퍼드 선교대학원에서 선교학 박사(Ph.D), 2세를 위한 〈오아시스교회〉개척 설립, 꿈을 이루는 선교 재단(Vision to Reality Foundation), 라이프기빙 사역(Lifegiving Ministry) 설립, 대표, 캄보디아 프놈펜 오아시스 하우스 카운슬링 센터 설립, 대표, Korean American Global Mission Association 대표, 킴넷 이사, 한국 키르케고르 연구소 대표, 캄보디아 로열 프놈펜국립대 철학 교수, 세계 64개국에서 1200번 이상 집회를 인도, 선교동원가, 저서로 시, 수필, 영문서적, 각종번역서 등 수십 권이 있다.

These are poems published in this book:

전율 외 2편
_ 캄보디아에서

오석환

나는 보았다
쓰레기통을 뒤져
아이스크림콘을
나누어서
빨아먹는 아이들

나는 들었다
이 콘이 더 맛있다
아냐 내것이 더 달아
어제 보다는 못하다
내일 다시 한 번 와보자

나는 느꼈다
까만 손가락에 끈적이는 아이스크림
지나가는 부잣집 아이의 손가락질
그들 근처에 못 가게 부티나는 아줌마의 눈길
끈적거리는 손을 더 까만 옷에 닦으며
땅바닥을 내려 보는 어린 마음들

나는 보고 듣고 느끼고
전율하며 울고 있다

망각

어느 날 나는
그리워야할 것들이
하나둘씩 없어지고 있음에
놀랐다

더 이상 기억하지
않으려고
버린 추억의 사진들
그리고 글 들이
가을 낙엽 쌓이듯
수북하다

길게 드리워진
망각의 그림자

여행 중 그리웠던 엄마도
소중했던 친구들도
그리움의 대상이 아닌
망각의 대상이 되었으니

나는 그리워한 것들이
하나씩 둘씩 없어지고 있음을
망각하였다

9/14-20: Korea tip

The best coffe I ever had in my life at the Sam Coffee shop in Korea – Yemen Mocha Mattari! Wow!!

Yemen mocha mattari
the Sam

The Mocha coffee bean is a variety of coffee bean originally from Yemen. It is harvested from the coffee-plant species Coffea arabica, which is native to Yemen. In appearance it is very small, hard, round with an irregular shape, and olive green to pale yellow in color. The name "Mocha" comes from the port of Mocha (al-Mukhā) through which most Yemeni coffee was exported before the 20th century. As of 1911, it was mostly exported via Aden and Hodeida. The central market for Yemeni coffee is at Bayt al-Faqih, about 140 km north of Mocha, and the coffee is grown in the mountain districts of Jabal Haraz, al-Udayn (sometimes written Uden), and Ta'izz, to the east.

9/15: LCT – Part A completed!
Jenny giving the devotion and our first time LCT done in Khmer Part A graduates! God si so good.

9/15: In Memoriam: Professor Sang Hyun Lee.

Princeton Theological Seminary shares with great sadness the passing of Sang Hyun Lee PhD, LHD (Hon.), DD (Hon.), Kyung-Chik Han Professor of Systematic Theology Emeritus. Professor

Lee passed away on Monday, September 4, 2023. Lee was a celebrated scholar, teacher, mentor, and the first Asian American faculty member at Princeton Seminary, after joining the faculty in 1980.

In the 30 years that followed, Lee was instrumental in the formation of the Asian American Program (AAP) and served as its director. AAP went on to become a leading voice and hub for the teaching and scholarship of Asian American theology and has evolved to become Princeton Seminary's Center for Asian American Christianity. Today, the Center is not only a nucleus for scholarship, but also offers innovative conferences, yearly forums, and leadership development for those in the community.

"The legacy that Dr. Lee leaves behind here at PTS and the wider theological academy is extraordinary," says Ki Joo (KC) Choi, Kyung-Chik Han Professor of Asian American Theology. "The AAP (and its present iteration as the Center for Asian American Christianity) would not exist were it not for his tireless dedication to the seminary and its students. Dr. Lee reminded all of us in theological education why Asian American voices matter in the struggle for justice in both church and society. We continue his legacy by doing the same, by working tirelessly to uplift those who have yet to be heard, by continuously expanding our circles of affection."

A distinguished scholar, Lee was best known for his ground-breaking book, From a Liminal Place: An Asian American Theology (2010). Among his other publications, Lee was also the editor of The Princeton Companion to Jonathan Edwards (2005) and author of The Philosophical Theology of Jonathan Edwards (1988).

"Professor Sang Hyun Lee was arguably the most important interpreter of Jonathan Edwards of his generation," says John R. Bowlin, Dean and Vice President of Academic Affairs. "He was also a serious and learned scholar of Christian doctrine and a profound and original theologian in his own right. But note well, Professor Lee's legacy endures not only through his scholarship, but also through the students he taught, the dissertations he directed, and the pastors and scholars he helped form. He will be dearly missed."

9/15: Aladin Used Book store visit

Aladin Used Book Store: Over 100,000 books!

9/15: Joyful Church Friday Night service.I had

I had such an incredible time ministering to Joyful Church again! They blessed me with so much love and financial support!

9/16: Unplanned meeting at SaeRom Church.

Pastor Lee walks into the Starbucks coffee shop while I was meeting Sister Kim. What?! How did you know we were meeting here? He did not know. He drove 3 hours from Saejeong City to Hanam City to attend SaeRom Church service and came to Starbucks next to the church. We had such a wonderful fellowship. God is amazing!

9/16: SaeRom Church leadership training.

I led a Revival meeting at SaeRom Church with Pastor Yom in February this year. I met Pastor Yom at Berendo Baptist Church in Los Angeles in 1986. She served as a children's minister and I was in charge of English ministry and Korean college group. After completing her education,

she came back to Korea and ended up planting a church at Ha Nam City. I ended up preaching one hour per session and many have received a gift of tongue at the end of our service. God is so good!

I ended up praying for all the young people in the church! They are so precious!

199

9/17: Ordinary Church - 2PM English service

Although church name was 'Ordinary Church' it was filled with extra-ordinary people!

9/18-19: Trip to Gangneung, Korea
I am visiting the Coffee Captial of Korea - Article titled, "1st generation barista Park Yi-Choo. "100 cups a day for 34 years. Coffee is still hard." (The JoonAng Daily Article on Oct. 2, 2022).

Gangneung is coffee. Starbucks is the main character who changed our taste buds, which were accustomed to "dabang coffee" and "vending machine coffee" instant americano, but Gangneung, Gangwon-do, spread the hand drip (brewing coffee) culture across the country. In the 2000s, roastery cafes began to be established in Gangneung, where beans are roasted and lowered one by one, and in about 20 years, it has become the center of Korean coffee with more than 450 cafes. Anmok Port (Gangneung Port), which used to be only a small port, is now connected to the nationwide coffee street, and the Gangneung Coffee Festival, which started in 2009, has established itself as a large festival enjoyed by more than 200,000 people every year. Prior to the opening of the 14th Gangneung Coffee Festival (October 7-10), we will introduce four famous people and unique cafes that led Gangneung's coffee culture. The first order is Park Yi-chu, who is called the first-generation barista in Korea, as the owner of "Bohemian" in Gangneung.

"As time goes by year, I think that people are more important than coffee. Doesn't the true value change depending on the drinker. One day it's sweet, another day it's bitter. It's like life."

These are the words of CEO Park Yi-chu (73), a master of Gangneung coffee. He has been on the road to coffee for more than 30 years, but making coffee is still the most difficult in the world. Coffee doesn't have the right answer like our lives. So even today, when he has gray hair, he roasts beans, make coffee, and try to sit face to face with more people.

People call him the 'first generation of last remaining coffee' and the 'legendary barista'. CEO Park Yi-chu is one of the "One West, Three Nights (the late Seo Jung-dal, the late Park Won-jun, Park Sang-hong, and Park Yi-chu)" who have promoted hand drip culture in Korea since the 1980s, and is the only active person. In the 2000s, when his cafe "Bohemian" was established in Gangneung, coffee culture took root on the east coast, which was no different from a coffee barren land. Bohemian, where you can taste his coffee, is still a sacred place among coffee lovers.

The business was great success, but the city life that was hit by people gradually became inflamed. Gangneung was the place that came to mind while looking for a quiet place. In July 2000, it opened a store next to the Jingogae Rest Area in Pyeongchang, and in October 2002, it moved to the old hotel Hyundai in Gyeongpodae, Gangneung, and in 2004, it built a nest inside Yeongok-myeon, Gangneung. (It currently has four direct stores, including the "Bohemian Roasters Park Yi-chu Coffee Factory" in Sacheon, Gangneung. The Gyeongpo store is run by his son Park Tae-chul, a barista).

9/18: Korean Kierkegaard Research Center board meeting

I had to be in Korea for this reason. We were having our first board meeting for Søren Kierkegaard Research Center for Korea. We had such a wonderful time at Young Jin Sashimi Restaurant, hosted by elder Oh and his wife.

9/19: Coming back to Cambodia.

During our Søren Kierkegaard Research Center board meeting I was notified that my friend Mike is in a critical condition. I was excused from the meeting. I took KTX to Seoul Train Station and from ther another KTX to the Inchon Airport and took a night flight to Phnom Penh.

9/20: My friend's life as a birthday gift

My friend Mike survived another breathing comma and I was able to share the gospel again with him.

By this time he really couldn't recognize me but I believe he could hear me so I spent much time talking to him about good old days since we were 12 years old.

9/20: Sand Tray therapy at Oasis House[4]

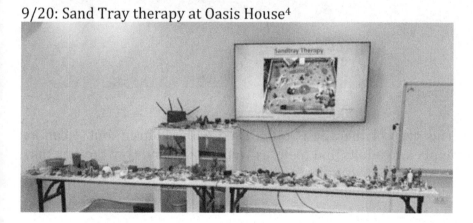

Sand tray therapy is a form of expressive therapy that is sometimes referred to as sandplay therapy (although sandplay does have a different approach) or the World Technique. It was

---

[4] https://tinyurl.com/22khaend. Accessed on 20 Sep. 2023.

developed by Margaret Lowenfeld, Dora Kalff, Goesta Harding, Charlotte Buhler, Hedda Bolgar, Lisolotte Fischer, and Ruth Bowyer.

This type of therapy is often used with children, but it can be applied to adults and teens as well. While sand tray therapy may be applied in couples and group settings, sandplay therapy is meant for individuals.

Sand tray therapy allows a person to construct their own microcosm using miniature toys and colored sand. The scene created acts as a reflection of the person's own life and allows them the opportunity to resolve conflicts, remove obstacles, and gain acceptance of self.

SAND TRAY THERAPY TECHNIQUES

The humanistic approach is a common strategy applied in sand tray therapy. Clinicians who use this technique rely solely on the client to find solutions to their problems, using the sand as a tool for healing. Through creative expression, a person in therapy is able to manifest in sand the things they would otherwise not be able to vocalize or address in traditional therapy. The therapist treats the person as whole and healed, knowing that the process of sand tray therapy allows the person to find the answers that are already within them.

9/21: Academia Response on downloading.

I found out today that people were leaving me messages on why they are down loading my books and papers. I am so honored that they want to read and study my papers and books!

- V. V. from Cambodia left a reason for downloading A Reflection on the Influence of the Church Growth Movement in Cambodia (2028 words). Dear professor, I have downloaded. This will help me in my pastor cell group. Thanks for sharing. God bless you!

- M. H. from USA left a reason for downloading Cambodia Research & Resource Center: Research Publication 2020 - Ministry to Khmer in the USA.

- K. J. from Korea left a reason for downloading Dr. Bob Oh's Poetry on Chun Sang Byung and Søren Kierkegaard. Dear,Thanks to your kindness, I got the paper on Poet Bob Oh!

- L. H. W. from Korea left a reason for downloading Commentary: Lamentations. I can read the commentary on Lamentations while listening to his Daily Gospel.

- S. M. from America (A Micro and Small Business Entrepreneurship) left a reason for downloading Dr. Bob

Oh's 21 Days of Fasting and Prayer. A sermon you gave at our church

- J. M. an Independent Researcher & Student, left a reason for downloading The Christian Life. You did Great work sir. thank you.

- Y. B. M. from Cambodia left a reason for downloading on Patron Client paper. Thank you for this paper.

- N. S. left a reason for downloading Dr Bob Oh's Lecture: Tithing (English and Korean Edition) - Thank you so much for your book on Tithing.

- J. P. of Korea wrote: Are there more videos of your Christian Framework series? I hope to see more! Thank you for sharing! I'm so blessed by you and Jenny!

- K. O. of Nigeria left a reason for downloading Dr. Bob Oh's Lecture: PhD Research Induction School Notes - Dear Robert, I listened to your presentation of your story after your PhD award at the OCMS chapel. The mobilization of funds and partnership across the USA with power Bike was amazing and terrific. Looking forward to contacting you by email. How are the school and ministries in Cambodia?

9/21: Visiting Little Red Fox Expresso Café

3. The Little Red Fox Espresso

⬤⬤⬤⬤⬤ 792 reviews · Closed Today
Coffee & Tea, Cafe · $$ - $$$ · 🍴 Menu ↗

"This place however is a little gem! Great service, good food, best coffee in..."
"Best coffee shop in town. What else?"

The Little Red Fox Espresso opened late 2014 with a simple vision to bring what we love about Australian cafe culture to Siem Reap then shake it all up with we love about Cambodia!

Our vision for the cafe was to create a space that is uniquely enjoyable for our customers and obviously our amazing team.

Since the beginning we have continued to drive our focus towards many community projects. Music, art and film (both national and international) have featured heavily in our journey. Some of our favorite memories include the week long music festival 'Chubmet' in 2017. Also, catering for the film 'First They Killed My Father' directed by Angelina Jolie for NETFLIX.

Furthermore, The Little Red Fox Espresso focuses on up-skilling, educating and training those who otherwise would not normally get the opportunity to learn management skills, our team is taught through the practice and freedom of creativity.

In addition, we are big on socially responsible and environmental business practices. Sharing that knowledge with our team in addition to always looking to better ourselves along the way.

Finally, The Little Red Fox Espresso is not a NGO or a Social Enterprise. However, we are a business which is passionate about advocating for what is right, both in our cafe and in our community.

Ratings and reviews

5.0 ●●●●● 792 reviews

#4 of 65 Coffee & Tea in Siem Reap

Travelers' Choice 2022

RATINGS

🍴 Food ●●●●○

🍽 Service ●●●●○

🛍 Value ●●●●○

🛈 Atmosphere ●●●●●

The Little Red Fox Espresso is the dream of long-term mates Adam Rodwell & David Stirling who wanted to bring their passion for Australian cafe culture to Siem Reap and meld it together with the truly unique Cambodian spirit.

No cafe experience can be better than the experience its team has day to day.

In our Den, we make decisions as a team with how we run The Little Red Fox Espresso. Furthermore, we ensure that each choice has a positive ethical and environmental impact. It is undoubtedly the best of coincidences that good hospitality choices – those that are good for our land and people, for the environment, for the body and mind – are also delicious and enjoyable.

The Little Red Fox Espresso team's talents are diverse, however, we're united by one thing: an overarching passion for creating a special space that melds our cultures together to create a truly unique environment for our guests.

9/22: The Source Café

This Café is ranked #2 in Siem Reap.   Coffe was OK but atmosphere was very classy!

9/22: Jenny's first Webinar lecture in Oct. 5.

Jenny was chosen as one of the keynote speakers for Asia Christian Counselors Association Webinar in Oct. 2023!

So proud of her and what she is accomplishing through her work as an inner healing counselor and as the director of Oasis House.

She is raising a next-generation Christian counselors in Cambodia and preparing for them to become the teachers to the teachers! They are in the multiplication mode which is really fantastic!

9/23: Good news from Ghana.

Hello Dr. Oh,
Thank you for your prayer support and encouragement. We were in the hospital to see the Renal Specialist who asked me to perform some laboratory tests. I am happy to announce that, he confirmed to me that there has been a lot of improvement according to my lab reports. He booked me for another appointment in the near future. Thanks a lot for your help.

Stay blessed,

C. A.

9/24: My 62ⁿᵈ birthday celebration begins!

Celebrating my Forever 41 birthday with my favorite wife at Dino Cafe, also my favorite cafe in Cambodia! Thank you all for your birthday wishes! Lord bless, and have a wonderful Sunday! I put this photo and text at my Facebook and so many responded with blessing! PTL!

- Happy birthday to professor! I wish you the best of happiness!!! Lord bless!
- Happy Birthday Lokru Robert Oh
- Happy Birthday young man!
- Happy Birthday Big Brother
- you forever are an example of faith and joy to us following behind
- Love you Bishop Happy Happy Birthday! What a blessing you are to us! Such a blessing and gift to the BODY of JESUS!!!!

Chelsea Ling
Happy birthday Pastor Bob!
Love Reply 6h

Nit Eldonai
Blessings birthday pastor 🙏🎂
Love Reply 6h

Elizabeth Kim
Happy Birthday!!! 😊
Love Reply 6h

Top Prum
May God richly bless you abundantly
Love Reply 6h

Monira Meas
Happy birthday to you Pastor 🎂🎉🎈
Love Reply 6h

Nakry Soeur
Happy birthday 🎂
Love Reply 6h

Piseth Path
Happy anniversary Pastor 🎂🎂🎉🎉
Love Reply 6h

David Von Bastes
Not too far from my age. 😄 Happy birthday pastor **Robert**
Love Reply 6h

Michalithgow Yaegashi
생일 축하합니다
Happy Birthday Big Brother
＼(^.^)
Love Reply 6h

Esther Chun
Happy birthday, pastor Oh!
Love Reply 6h
↳ Samin Lee replied · 1 Reply 6h

Jin Han Rim
Congratulations 🎉
Love Reply 6h

Bophal Yos - Maher
Happy birthday Pastor 🎉🎂
Love Reply 5h

Sharon Khoo
Happy Birthday indeed! Blessed celebrating & Heaven's blessings on you always!
🎉🎂
Love Reply 5h

ស្រុក ព្រែក ✔
Happy birthday pastor 🙏🙏
Love Reply 5h

Nathan Cho
Happy Birthday 🎉
Love Reply 5h

Nith Chea
Happy birthday to you pastor
Love Reply 5h

Pamela Jourden
happy birthday my Bishop
Love Reply 5h

Pamela Jourden
you forever are an example of faith and joy to us following behind
Love Reply 5h

Sung-Hun Kim
Happy birthday to Bishop Oh! Have a great day.
Love Reply 5h

Narantsatsral Sharav
Happy birthday pastor
Many more blessings
🎉🎉🎂

Love Reply 5h

Hyepin Im
Happy birthday 🎂
Love Reply 5h

Ny Sophors
Congratulations 💜🤍🙏🙏
Love Reply 5h

Seangly Leng
Happy birthday to you pastor. May God bless you and your wife. Thank you for your heart for Cambodian people. We love your heart.
Love Reply 4h

Judy Hong
Happy Birthday Pastor Oh!
Love Reply 4h

Brian Jourden
Love you Bishop Happy Happy Birthday! What a blessing you are to us! Such a blessing and gift to the BODY of JESUS!!!!
Love Reply 4h

Grace R. Dyrness
Happiest of birthdays Bob!
Love Reply 4h

Chan Vanneth
Blessed birthday to you Handsome Pastor 🙏🙏💜💜
Love Reply 4h

Steve Seonghoon Kang
amen 😊
Love Reply 4h

Sam W Scaleb
Blessed birthday
Love Reply 4h

Peter Rock N Vanneth
You are My Favorite Pastor 🙏🙏 ···
Happy Birthday 🎉🎂🎈🎁🎉🎂🎈🎁🎉🎂🎈🎁
🎉🎂🎈🎁🎉🎂🎈🎁🎉🎂🎈🎁
🎉🎂🎈🎁🎉🎂🎈🎁🎉🎂🎈🎁
🎉🎂🎈🎁🎉🎂🎈🎁🎉🎂🎈🎁
Love Reply 4h

David Taejong Lee
생일축하드립니다 감사
Love Reply 4h

Roger Kim
Happy birthday!!! 😊
Love Reply 4h

Young Lee
Happy Birthday! 😊
Love Reply 4h

Sombor Tha
Happy birthday Pastor
HAPPY Birthday
Love Reply 4h

Sarah Lee
Happy Birthday, Pastor Bob!
Love Reply 4h

Satya Green
Happy anniversary!
Love Reply 4h

Eric Beck
Happy birthday pastor! May God continue to work greatly in you and through you!
Love Reply 4h

Ky Viseth Sambath
Happy Anniversary Pastors, all the best blessings
Love Reply 3h

Layvin Chea
Happy birthday pastor 🙏🙏🎉
Love Reply 3h

Aly Nuon
May God bless you both Pastor 💜💜

JBerinai
Blessed Birthday to you!
Love Reply 22h

Heang Socheat
Happy birthday pastor May God bless you
Love Reply 22h Edited

Shirley Kim
Happy Birthday!
Like Reply 22h

Piotr Tatar
Happy Birthday, Pastor Robert! Every blessing!
Love Reply 22h

Sarah Faith Song
Happy Birthday pastor
Love Reply 21h

John Kim
밀리샤니아 생신을 진심으로 축하드립니다. 목사님!!!
Love Reply 21h

Sam Son
Happy
Love Reply 21h

Julie Ma
Enjoy the celebration!
Love Reply 20h

Ingun Kang
Happy Birthday to you~ dear Rev. Oh!! Love and prayers~
Love Reply 19h

Nget Sakny
Happy birthday, pastor! May God bless you and be with you. He gives you strength, good health, and longevity for the Kingdom of God.
Love Reply 2h

Vanna Chum
Love Reply 2h

Ben Choe
Happy birthday!
Love Reply 2h

Va Vachna
happy birthday prof!
Love Reply 1h

Bunny Sun
Happy Birthday Pastor, Blessings!!!
Love Reply 1h

Eleanor Sebiano
Happy Birthday Much blessings
Love Reply 31m Edited

Rani Eunyoung Ko
목사님 생신축하드립니다..
Love Reply 22m

Greg Paek
Happy Birthday. Are you sure it's 41st? It's not 14th?
Love Reply 21m

Jeannette Gaïtou-Baas
Happy blessed birthday!
Love Reply 18h

Apple Sirichai
Happy Birthday!
Love Reply 17h

Paul Devadhass Ponnusamy

Jason Kim
Happy bday P. Oh!
And you have the same bday as Jamie Jungah Kim! Guess I won't be forgetting your bday either. lol
Reply 16h

Julie Yu
Happiest birthday pastor Bob! You are aging backwards! Share your secret!
Love Reply 16h
Robert Oh replied · 1 Reply

Samoeun Intal

Shanti Adeline Abishegam
Birthday blessings, Robert.

Bill Prevette
Happy Birthday Robert. You and Jenny look happy! Soon you will be 27!
Love Reply 15h

- Happy birthday God's servant. May you receive the grace of forever green. Congratulations!!!!
- Birthday blessings & marvelous joy, Pastor Robert.
- May the Lord Jesus bless you

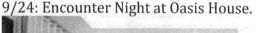

- Happy Birthday Robert. You and Jenny look happy! Soon you will be 27!
- Happiest birthday pastor Bob! You are aging backwards! Share your secret!
- Happy birthday, pastor! May God bless you and be with you. He gives you strength, good health, and longevity for the Kingdom of God.
- Happy birthday pastor! May God continue to work greatly in you and through you!

9/24: Encounter Night at Oasis House.

God showed up and ministered to so many young people! PTL! But I heard the news that Mike is once again in a critical condition so I had to pack one more time to fly out in the morning. I visited Siem Reap 4 times this month! On top of that Steve from USA is coming. I was scheduled to host him for a week at Phnom Penh. Thank God Missionary Kim's Timothy center could host him and welcome him as their English teacher.

213

9/26: Mike went to heaven at 6:30 AM!
We scheduled to have a final service for Mike and take the breathing tube out at 10 AM – but by 6:30 AM I got a call telling me that he passed away!

Robert Oh
6m · 🌐

···

Thanks for your prayer! My friend Mike passed away on Sep. 26th, TUE, at 6:30AM. I believe I will see him in heaven, since he did respond to the gospel on his death bed. His body is now in Phnom Penh, waiting for the American Embassy to give permission for cremation. Sharing a photo of Mike when we were having a noodle lunch near my home in Phnom Penh!

I did not want to share a photo of him on his death bed. This photo will remind me of our friendship of 50 years! See you in heaven Mike!

6/27: A real sad news of Karl's death by heart attack!

Robert Oh
Just now ·

...

Sad news! My riding buddy friend (One with his thumbs up) passed away with a heart attack in the USA last weekend. We traveled through many parts of the USA and Mexico as riding partners! We will miss him greatly! (Photo: We were on 10 days trip to Baja, Mexico).

From Michael's FaceBook post:

My best friend and motorcycle riding buddy Karlos Guevara Park passed away last weekend in Oregon due to a heart attack while he was driving down from Seattle on PCH to visit family and friends in SF and LA. I can not believe it and am so sad. He called me last Friday night while he was in Oregon to talk about getting together in LA this Thursday and staying over at my house.

Karl and I attended the same elementary school in Seoul, Korea, and we met again when we attended UC Berkeley. We became best friends and riding buddies during the last five years, and we went on riding trips all over North America, including last year's ride to Newfoundland, Canada. Karl was the one who got me into adventure motorcycle riding and trips. He loved his family, friends, food, travels, ocean, nature, places, and people of all kinds. He had the biggest heart of anyone I

know who loved being on the road. He died doing what he loved, which he once told me is not a bad way to go. I have lost a best friend and riding buddy. We had so many wonderful memories together. I will miss him dearly.

(Michael is the one in the middle).

6/29: Missionary Bernard Kuh goes to heaven.
I worked with him first on the Navajo Mission project in 1992. He was a CPA at the time and gave me great insight about preparing for our financial future. I will miss you Dr. Kuh!

Professor Timothy Park of Fuller wrote on his FaceBook: Fuller alumnus Pastor Dr. Bernard Kuh, who has been battling gallbladder cancer, is awaiting the end of his life at Redland Community Hospital. Please pray that he may go to the Lord in peace. His hospital room is room 5108. And the following day: Dr. Bernard Kuh is gone to be with the Lord this morning at 9:50 at Redland Community Hospital. Sorry that we cannot see him again on this earth. He has been deeply involved in developing workers for the kingdom of God and gospel in Indochina Peninsular including Vietnam and Cambodia.

My September Schedule page as an art form: This may become a collector's item 100 years later!

217

October

October was originally the eighth month. Octagon, octopus… most words that begin with the Latin prefix "Oct" have some connection to the number eight. But what about October? While the modern calendar considers the autumn month to be the 10th of the year, it wasn't always that way. For the ancient Romans, who created the earliest form of the calendar we use now, October was originally the eighth month.

Today's calendar follows a 12-month cycle, though the earliest iterations only had 10 months. In ancient Rome, the year began in March and ran through December, with the first four months named for Roman deities. The next six months had more straightforward, numerical names that referenced their place in the year. The remaining weeks of winter (which would eventually become January and February) were largely ignored on paper; when the harvest season ended, so did the calendar, until the next spring planting season rolled around.

Over time, the calendar expanded by two months; January and February were added around 700 BCE, and by about the middle of the fifth century BCE, they had become the starting months of the year. When Julius Caesar introduced the Julian calendar, he didn't adjust the number-named months to more appropriate places, though later Roman emperors tried, using names that didn't stick.

10/1: Living Like Kierkegaard – Sep. 2023 is published!

Robert Oh

Living Like Kierkegaard: September 2023

Living Like Kierkegaard: September 2023
Paperback
by Robert Oh (Author)

See all formats

Kindle
$5.35
You Earn: 17 pts
Read with Our Free App

Report incorrect product information.

Language	Dimensions	ISBN-13	
EN English	6.0 x 0.5 x 9.0 inches	979-8862917529	See all details

10/1: Hosting Steve from USA!

I was at Steve's Coin Laundry business in LA several months ago. He says, "I made a promise to God to visit Cambodia 5 times but I visited only 4 times!" I said, "Well, Covid is over and you can come over anytime now!" And he did! Only problem was that 3 friends of mine passed away last week and I was so busy taking care of cremation / funeral process for Mike I had absolutely no time for Steve. He served at Timothy Center of Phnom Penh Thmey. Thank God he enjoyed his time teaching English to young people. On his last day at Cambodia, I took him to Aeon Mall II of Sen Sok. Steve was impressed and I was happy to see him so happy! He promised to come back to Cambodia either next year of in 2025.

10/1: Encounter House Sunday worship at Oasis House

Encounter House now holds its regular Sunday service at Oasis House! We are so happy we can be part of this beautiful ministry each week. PTL!

10/2: LCT Devotion & teaching!
I led LCT morning devotion today. Jenny also taught and teachers from all over came and blessed our Khmer students!

10/2: Dinner with LCT teachers
Gill and Sharon came from Thailand to bless our LCT students. Jenny and I took them to our favorite Chinese restaurant and had a feast!

10/3: Start my 4k swimming gain.

September was cruel! Took away about 20 days from living a normal life. I realized the first thing that I sacrificed was swimming time. So this morning I got up and told myself, "Bob, shut up and just go to the pool and swim 90 minutes without making any excuses!" So I did that – PTL! It wasn't the best time at 2'28" per 100 meter but it was done!

10/3: Dr. Phillip Cha found me at Academia!

ACADEMIA

Phillip Cha started following you

In 1986 Phillip was prt of the college department at Bernedo Baptist Church. He now is a licensed Marriage and Family Therapist working in San Frnacisco area. On his FaceBook post the following was posted: This two-part workshop series aims to address the critical but neglected issue of race-based trauma among Asian American men particularly of East Asian origin such as Korea, Japan, and China. It will suggest some practical strategies to promote wellness and empowerment using the principles of Acceptance and Commitment Therapy (ACT). ACT is a non-pathologizing approach to therapy and skills building that emphasizes mindful acceptance and meaningful action rather than symptom reduction. This approach, alternatively known as Acceptance and Commitment Training, can also be utilized in non-clinical settings (e.g., church, temple) by practitioners who are not necessarily therapists (e.g., ministers, coaches, etc.)

Acceptance and Commitment Training is very compatible with indigenous Asian wellness practices such as mindfulness, acceptance, and compassion/wisdom traditions and can be well-suited for individuals who are less likely to seek mental health services due to stigma. When used in conjunction with communal support within an intersectional framework, ACT can be an effective approach for addressing racial trauma among Asian American men.

10/4: Cremation of Mike at Phnom Penh

 After having tons of problems with the US Embassy and the funeral home, we finally were able to conduct a cremation service for my friend Mike. It was unreal to see his body in a wooden coffin and see his body become ash as wood burns and the smoke rises to heaven. Goodbye my friend! We will see each other in heaven next to our Lord Jesus!

One of the recent intercessor I met in Korea sent the following Email which comforted me greatly:

Hello Pastor Robert,
I hope you're doing well. I wasn't sure whether I should share but I submit this to you. As I was praying for your friend before he passed away, I saw God stamping a cross on his for head and this cross was made out of light, shining from his forehead like a spotlight. It was so bright.

I believe God has chosen him and he is with Him in heaven. I was encouraged by God's heart for your friend and I hope you are too. May God bless you and your ministry!

223

10/5: My personal record 4k swim under 90 minutes!

I am so happy to report that I broke my personal record of swimming 4k under 90 minutes today. Last time was 2'28" per 100 meter, but today I swam in 2'11" per 100 meter – PTL!

I need to swim as much as possible before going to Korea because I would not have a pool available during my stay in Korea. I will be walking though. Need to be in shape!

10/5: Jenny's Webinar for ACCA Conference

Jenny will be the speaker for Asian Christian Counseling Association Webinar 2023 – PTL! I found the following information about ACCA:

Benefits of Belonging to ACCA:
ACCA is composed of member nations not individual people. Individuals within nations are members of their respective National Association which is a member of ACCA. Benefits exist bilaterally –

224

for individual nations who join ACCA and for ACCA when each nation joins.

Benefits For Your Nation:
Solidarity, Support and Encouragement. It is pioneering work to develop a national association. ACCA is keen to support, encourage, and build long-term relationships with those people choosing to do so. There is power in connecting for inspiration, collaboration, and cooperation, whether in terms of leadership of associations, and/or seeing what other Christian counselling practitioners really do.

Bi-annual ACCA Regional Conference: This offers opportunities to participate in training, share resources, networking, fellowship and encouragement, in the area of integration of Christian faith and counselling – including integration of psychology, theology, spirituality, and missions, at lay pastoral and professional counsellor level. The ACCA vision is to empower the Asian church in all its depth and breadth, (including pastors and counsellors) to assist people grow and overcome mental and psychological issues.

Mentoring: ACCA Member nations offer mentoring to those nations who are hoping to develop national Christian Counselling Associations.

Guidelines: ACCA seeks to share experience regarding national counselling association's development and accreditation processes where helpful. (for example ethics or policy guidelines, which may be adapted to suit national conditions).

Resources: ACCA hopes to foster development and sharing of relevant training and resources specifically for Asia.
Prayer: Join the regular monthly prayer meeting hosted by a different nation each time praying for national associations, their people, growth, development, impact, and activities.

Benefits For ACCA:

Asian Region Policy Making: Nominated national representatives on the ACCA Board together shape the future direction of Christian counselling in Asia.

Alignment and Refinement: ACCA offers a platform to review and develop our Christian counselling approach and methodologies arising from sharing best practices and innovative strategies that respond well to the changing environment and mindsets of the Asian people.

Shared Ministry Opportunities: From time to time these opportunities arise across professional groups, nations, and around the region.
Fellowship and mutual encouragement: In ACCA we seek to spur each other onwards towards effectively serving the Kingdom of God both nationally and regionally in Asia, as a community of people-helpers with a common objective and mission.

10/7: My friend Karl's funeral announcement.

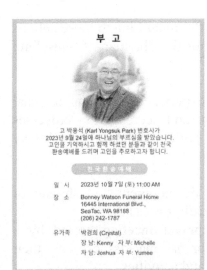

Kenny Park (Son) wrote: Karlos Guevara Park beloved husband, father, uncle, brother, and friend, passed away on 9/24/23 in Brookings, OR while on one of his many adventures. Karl was a free-spirited and adventurous soul who lived life to the fullest. He loved exploring the world, meeting new people, and trying new things. He was also a loving and devoted husband, father, and friend to many. We've lost a beautiful and inspiring person who will be deeply missed.

Karl, I wish I had our final meeting with you in LA like we planned! I will miss you especially during our riding trips with Mike Yang!

10/8: Encounter House Sunday worship

So happy my missionary friends came and joined our worship service. Thank you Jesus!

She goes to the church this morning

I got a great news that Mok, my friend Mike's wife, joined Siem Reap New Life Church. I got this photo report from Pastor Samkol and his wife this morning. PTL! What a wonderful testimony to a very sad news on my friend passing!

10/9: Breakfast with John the Baptist Church crew.

can be planted in Cambodia.

Missionary Yang brought his disciple for last 16 years who became the pastor of John the Baptist Church. It's so wonderful to witness a healthy church being planted and leadership given over to the local pastors. I pray that more churches like this one

10/9: Lunch with COP kids (I mean adults).

They wanted to treat us for Jenny's August birthday and my September birthday in October. We went to Jenny's favorite vegetarian restaurant in Phnom Penh.

10/9: Dinner with RUPP Philosophers.

I had another meal meeting at dinner with Royal University of Phnom Penh philosophy students. We were celebrating Socrates' second master degree from Japan!

10/10: CRRC meeting at ICCHI building.

Missionary Chang finished his research center – Cambodia Church History Institute. I am so happy we started CRRC together 10 years ago and still going strong in our relationship and partnership in research.

10/12: To Korea with Jenny

Jenny and I arrived on 11th of October and next day we met up with Oasis House crew for wonderful lunch! Lina was invited to speak at Korea and she brought her friends from Oasis House.

10/13: Pchum Bun of Cambodia.

According to Wikipedia, Pchum Bun, lit. "balled rice gathering" (or

Pchum Bun

Prayers during Pchum Bun

Ancestor's Day) is a Cambodian 15-day religious festival, culminating in celebrations on the 15th day of the tenth month in the Khmer calendar, at the end of the Buddhist Lent, Vassa. In 2023, Pchum Bun will begin on October 13 and end on October 16.

The day is a time when many Cambodians pay their respects to deceased relatives of up to 7 generations. Buddhist monks chant the suttas in Pali language overnight (continuously, without sleeping) in prelude to the gates of hell opening, an event that is presumed to occur once a year, and is linked to the cosmology of King Yama. During this period, the gates of hell are opened and spirits of the ancestors are presumed to be especially active. In order to liberate them, food-offerings are made to benefit them, some of them having the opportunity to end their period of purgation, whereas others are imagined to leave hell temporarily, to then return to endure more suffering; without much explanation, relatives who are not in hell (who are in heaven or other realms of existence) are also generally expected to benefit from the ceremonies.

10/13: Space Jak Buffet Brunch.

Jenny and I really enjoy staying at HIPM in Korea. The only complaint Jenny had was that there wasn't a good breakfast place nearby. Well, we found this wonderful breakfast buffet nearby. Space Jak is developing cultural and artistic contents. Planning, acting on behalf of, and developing creative contents as they run Gallery and have art exhibition.

10/13: Agapao Friday night meeting

Jenny was ministering to Solomon's Porch Church of Korea and I ministered at Agapao Church. I am so happy everytime I preach here! Thank you Jesus!

10/14: Dinner with Yoo missionary couple.

I had a mission from my sister Somi. When she found out that I will be visiting the city of Yangjoo, she wanted me to deliver some Love Offering to her friends. Missionary Yoo is fighting cancer. I love their pure heart for the gospel and tenesity to preach the and teach the word of God.

10/15: Jenny - Inner Healing Meeting at Korea Solomon's Porch

Jenny ministered to eight people – each one hour and half long session over the weekend. They know her soft spot – food! Since Hong Kong Solomon's Porch Church days, sister Jiye was my chief intercessor, as a part of Bob's Angels. But now she moved to Seoul and loves to host Jenny at her apartment and have her ministered to all of her friends.

10/15: Jesus Power Church of Yangjoo.

I love Pastor Ryu who makes me look skinny standing next to him.

231

10/16: Epipodo publication celebration

Pastor Baek from USA came to Korea to celebrate Epipodo's 14th publication. I shared my passion for poetry and my journey as a poet with the rest of awesome Christian poets of Korea.

10/17: HIPM - special lecture

Jenny led an awesome lecture on Inner healing and HIPM crew made us a feast to remember!

10/18-20: Visiting Sejeong, Korea.

Jenny visited Sejeong city for the first time and met lovely people of Søren Kierkegaard Research Center leaders and decided to live in Sejeong city from next year – August and on. She will be applying for her dual citizenship. It will take anywhere from 6 months to 8 months! We might want to find a more permanent place at Sejong City so I can play the role of the director more fully and base our retirement years in Korea there.

10/21: Book Talk on Lily of the field of Søren Kierkegaard.

I posted my Book Talk on Søren Kierkegaard's book 'Lily of the field and bird in the air.' Scan the QR code and it will take you to my YouTube channel.

10/25: Used Book hunting day!

I love to go to hunt for used books! I spent some time at old bookstores today. Scan the QR code and it will take you to my YouTube channel.

10/20-22: Visiting Joomoonjin!

Jenny and I try to go to Joomoonjin every opportunity we get. Elder Oh couple are such wonderful supporters and friends for so many years. Their Sashimi Restaurant provides us with a feast every time.

We invited Pastor Samin of HIPM there. We had such agreat time there. I made our experience there into a short video.

Scan the QR code and it will take you to my YouTube channel.

10/22: Visiting Favor Church of Korea.

Pastor Woolim Ma of Philippine started a church plant in Korea. It was their second week and we were there. I shared a brief testimony and we had wonderful time of food and fellowship afterwards.

10/23: Lunch with Brian and Esther in Korea.

We planted the first Oikos Church in 1991 together. They were my Sunday School students at Berkland Baptist Church. In early 1980's as I prayed for them they both received the gift of tongue! PTL! It was good seeing them in Korea.

10/24: Lunch with my sisters!

Sister Nancy is visiting Korea from Mongolia for health reason and Sister Cindy was taking a vacation after her retirement. Thank God we can meet in Korea and celebrate God's goodness together! PTL!

10/27-28: Visiting Sejeong, Korea.

It was the last day for the Jon Stewart's book review class. I shared my vision and testimony about what we need to do with Søren Kierkegaard's books and teachings. It was so good to be with among Kierkegaardians' of Korea.

10/29: The Love Church at the city of Eechun.

I volunteered to go to this church. It took me 2 hours of train ride to get there but totally worth it. They are trying to plant a micro church. They ministered to kids in orphanage of Eechun and widows of the village. Prof. Bj of ACTS introduced this church to me last year and I fell in love with the Love Church! ☺

My October Schedule page as an art form: This may become a
collector's item 100 years later!

236

November

11/1: Living Like Kierkegaard: Oct. 2023 is published.

Living Like Kierkegaard: October 2023
Kindle Edition
by Robert Oh (Author)   Format: Kindle Edition

See all formats a

Kindle
$5.35
You Earn: 17 pts

Read with our free app

I want to 'live' like Søren Kierkegaard. I met too many people wanting to talk abc
existential philosophy but refusing to live as an existentialist! Most likely, Søren K
would not want to be identified as an existentialist, but he did start a philosophic
movement called 'existentialism.' Maybe we can just try to copy and try to live lik
Kierkegaard as just a Kierkegaardian!

11/1: KimNet zoom meeting & lunch.

It was 2023 final KimNet Board members' meeting via Zoom today. I have been running with these men and women for the last 20 years. Pray that KimNet will continue to serve its purpose. I am so thankful for meeting Pastor Samuel 20 years ago.

11/2: Email from Brian about Jonathan.

Greetings from the Kingdom! We are happy that our boy, Johnathan, just graduated from ACT High School (private school). Some of you know the atrocious birth narratives of each of our adopted children, and although they may not remember, their bodies remember. Both must work extremely hard to overcome abandonment and attachment issues. Simple things often take a lot of energy and will power. Although he was in the middle of his class, John worked very hard to get there. Kudos on John and thanks to Pastor Bob Oh who provided a scholarship each year.

11/4: Meeting spiritual mentors!

I met Pastor Samuel Choe (One wearing Kangol hat like me) 20 years ago at KimNet meeting. His wife Esther Mom asked me to be her spiritual son, so he became my spiritual Mom's husband! Later he claimed his spiritual fathership! ☺ Esther Mom passed away and Pastor Victoria has become his spiritual partner – PTL!

11/4: Meeting more spiritual mentors in one day!

Jenny and I met this wonderful couple in 1997 at Moscow, Russia. They were head of Grace Bible College and planted many churches in Siberia. It was so good to run into them at Grace Mission Center today! PTL!

11/4: Patty's Lexus donated.

When my sister Nancy went back to Mongolia, my last child received their 20 years old Lexus! Today Patty donated her Lexus to an organization (A silver one at the bottom) because it was giving her too much trouble. Instead of constantly fixing an old car, she gave it away. Lord now she needs a car! ☺

11/5: Catalyst Church Sunday service

I preached a message on 'the snail, the turtle and the bullet train!' In the message, I shared how I will be registered at the Guinness World Record for drinking 1000 cups of coffee in 64 countries! After the service this cute boy came up to me and said, "Now I know **anyone** can hold a Guinness World Record!"

11/6: Trip to N. Cal. Dinner with Kyungsuk

His wife Sanghee, whom Jenny and I knew since 1979, passed away and since we were in Cambodia, we couldn't attend her funeral. Then we heard that he had a minor stroke! We had to drive up to see him and make sure he is OK. He is the one who introduced me to the Amazon self-publishing. My life has not been same ever since that day. We treated him to a nice meal at "Jang Soo Jang' which means 'Live Long Life' in Korean. ☺

11/7: Half Moon Bay with Cindy Nunim.

My sister Cindy recently retired from her optometry practice and wanted to take a day trip to Half Moon Bay! What a beautiful day it was. We feasted on Sea food by the bay.

This is a short history of Half Moon Bay: Spanish town, or Half Moon Bay as it is now called, is perhaps the oldest settlement in San Mateo County, dating back to the 1840s. For thousands of years, the land was inhabited by Ohlone Indians. They lived in many places around San Mateo County, including Half Moon Bay's Pilarcitos Creek. Cabrillo Highway (Highway 1) and Highway 92 generally follow original Ohlone trails along the coast and over the mountains. In the 1840s, land grants were given to early Mexican settlers.

With the gold rush, Americans and others of many cultures soon followed. The early community became known as "Spanishtown" because of the number of Spanish speaking inhabitants there. In 1874, Spanishtown officially became known as Half Moon Bay, named for the beautiful crescent-shaped harbor that lies just north of town. As the late 1800s passed, the area's character became established by the diverse representation of cultures that made the Coastside a prime example of the American melting pot.

The 1906 earthquake destroyed Mexican adobes and some early American efforts to build brick business buildings in Half Moon Bay. Wooden homes and shops survived the quake, and many of those early wooden structures still remain.

In 1907, the Ocean Shore Railway was constructed along the shoreline from San Francisco to Tunitas Glen, just south of Half

Moon Bay. Due to financial problems and the increasing popularity of the horseless carriage, the railroad ceased operation in 1920.

The City of Half Moon Bay was incorporated in 1959. It is now a town of approximately 12,500 people. It has many reminders of its early beginnings in the mid-1800s as an agricultural town. Fields of flowers, artichokes, brussel sprouts, Christmas trees, pumpkins and other crops blanket the breathtaking landscape.

11/7: Dinner with Joe & Liz @ Sister Somi & Mike's home.

You know you are getting old when your nephew brings his wife to a family dinner and we ask, "So when are you going to have children?" A typical Korean uncle thing to say at a party!

11/7: Jenny's in the 'Living Wholeness' news!

Yes she is in the middle of the photo! I enlarged the photo for you.

11/8: Breakfast with Pastor Gil.
I met Gil at Cambodia ten years ago. He now serves at a local church in San Jose area. I found his bio at his church website:

 Gil Suh grew up in a Buddhist family in Korea and immigrated to the States as a teenager. Gil was baptized at the age of 19. After graduating from Biola University, Gil went to Calvin Theological seminary where he met his wife, Joyce (Scholten) from Canada. They moved to Nigeria and taught at a Bible school in a rural area for six years during which their three children were born.

Gil's family had to leave Nigeria unexpectedly due to tribal violence. After serving a congregation of young adults in San Jose, CA, for four years, they moved to Cambodia in 2008 to do the mission work of mentoring and training emerging leaders in Cambodia.

While Gil and Joyce were on "home leave" from their mission work, they visited San Jose Christian Reformed Church, their commissioning congregation. Gil preached at the church's first in-person worship service after the pandemic on Easter, 2021. The church was without a pastor at the time. Gil felt called to become the pastor of San Jose CRC to help them as they went through a process of discerning their future. He began his time at San Jose CRC in September, 2021.

Gil and Joyce Suh are both ordained ministers of Christian Reformed Church of North America (CRCNA). Joyce currently serves as the Global Area Director for Resonate Global Mission, the denominational mission agency of CRCNA. Gil likes playing basketball and tennis, and Joyce loves reading various novels. They both enjoy hiking.

San Jose Christian Reformed Church consists of people from every generation and from every walk of life who are being renewed by God's grace to join together in worship, community, and mission.

Grace—the gift of kindness from God that we don't deserve and cannot earn—is foundational to our beliefs, who we are, and what we do. Grace starts with God and is revealed throughout the Bible, clearly embodied in the life, death, and resurrection of his Son, Jesus Christ. However, grace doesn't end with God's work in the world. God's grace renews the Church to live a life of grace in the world. Thus, grace is our foundation and our mission in all that we are called to be and do in the world.

Our church was founded in 1953 by a group of people who had been moved by God's grace to start a Christian Reformed church in San Jose. As a larger body, San Jose Christian Reformed Church is part of the Christian Reformed Church in North America, which has about 300,000 people in the U.S. and Canada.

11/8: Berkeley & Top Dog

Jenny and I had to visit Berkeley in order to eat Top Dog. Here is a bit of history from their website: Sampling around for the best frankfurter to sell (and eat!) led to other fine sausages and the idea was born to offer them as hot dogs as well. When no right site could be found in S.F. or Sausalito, hello, Berkeley. That was 1966 and with the paint hardly dry we opened on —surprise— a home football game day. Fifteen minutes later it was full house madness. Talk about learning to host and cook on the run!

With such fans it's been interesting, often challenging — but fun. As in that boy's world, largely gone by, we continue to seek out the best sausage from the best sausage-makers who, born to a tradition of taste, we believe, tend to serve it better. Calabrese? How ya gonna top S.F.'s award-winning house of Molinari? Buon Gusto! Or that little Portuguese plant in San Leandro that makes but two products, one of which, the linguiça, we are proud to say, stands pork shoulder butt higher than any of its competitors in the Bay Area. Then there's the cooked bratwurst from Saag's — as authentic an old-world

European taste as you're likely to find. And from another quality

third generation producer, Schwarz of S.F., bockwurst unsurpassed! (The "top dog" says that in over fifty years and four continents, he's never tasted better.)

We remain evermore on the prrrowl for unique sausages for affordable and convenient hot dog enjoyment.

11/9: Søren Kierkegaard zoom meeting.

St. Olaf University hosted a zoom meeting on the topic on 'Mental Health Crisis.' It was led by Rene Rosfort of Kierkegaard Research Center of Copenhagen, Denmark.

It was very informative and well balanced lecture on Søren Kierkegaard's teaching on anxiety and current mental helath crisis – post Covid 19.

11/11: Oasis House Board Zoom meeting

Hum. I don't think I got their permission to post this here! ☺

I am so glad we can hold zoom meeting now and have people join from New York, England, Cambodia, and Northern California!

11/12: Preaching at Epipodo Christian Church!

This is a very small church with a very big heart for mission! They have been putting our mission work in Cambodia on their bulletin and have been praying for us for many years! Just for that, I try to visit as many times as possible each year to minister to these precious people. So thankful to Pastor Baek and his people for their faithfulness!

11/13: Surprise visit from my nieces!

We made uncle Bob burger – they are the buns and I am the meat in the middle!

11/15: Planning zoom meeting for July 2024.
Dr. Ma sent me an Email with the following request: One question: I am organizing the 2024 Scholars Consultation of Empowered 21 on "Fulfilling the Every ONE's Vision in the Context of Religions." Here is an idea: You team up with a Cambodian leader to produce a

study on Reaching Cambodian Buddhists and Travel to Jakarta for the Consultation (July 1-2). I immediately thought about Pastor Vachna of Cambodia to be part of this academic journey.

So I google scholar search the key terms 'Cambodia Church planting Buddhism' and 3 out of 5 entries were my publication! Wow! I am the expert on Cambodia church planting according to Google Scholar AI. ☺

Google Scholar — cambodia church planting buddhism

Articles · About 15,900 results (0.04 sec)

Any time
Since 2023
Since 2022
Since 2019
Custom range...

Sort by relevance
Sort by date

Any type
Review articles

include patents
✓ include citations

✉ Create alert

Patron-client relationship in cross-cultural church planting: a case study of Cambodia Bible College, 1998-2015
S Oh - 2019 - repository.mdx.ac.uk
... to understand why Cambodian churches planted by Korean missionaries in Cambodia are not ... Because of this passive attitude, Ravasco argues that Buddhism in Cambodia is more ...
☆ Save 🔊 Cite Cited by 1 Related articles All 3 versions

[PDF] **Patron-Client Relationship in Cross-cultural Church Planting: A Case Study of Cambodia Bible College**
SR Oh - core.ac.uk
... to understand why Cambodian churches planted by Korean missionaries in Cambodia are not ... Because of this passive attitude, Ravasco argues that Buddhism in Cambodia is more ...
★ Save 🔊 Cite Related articles

The Historical Interface between Buddhism and Christianity in Cambodia, with Special Attention to the Christian and Missionary Alliance, 1923–1970
B Wong - Buddhist-Christian Studies, 2020 - muse.jhu.edu
... of my research has been with Cambodian Christians, one ... to the Buddhist and Christian communities in Cambodia and ... the primarily Theravada nation of Cambodia in the first quarter of ...
☆ Save 🔊 Cite Cited by 2 Related articles All 6 versions

Emerging Christianity in Cambodia: People Movement to Christ or Playground for Global Christianity?
T Brandner - International Bulletin of Mission Research, 2020 - journals.sagepub.com
... organization dedicated to church planting and mission research, ... Furthermore, Cambodian Buddhism is permeated by ... -religious nature of Cambodian Buddhism and the disruption ...
☆ Save 🔊 Cite Cited by 3 Related articles All 3 versions

[PDF] **The Role of Patron as Father in Church Planting Efforts in Cambodia.**
R Oh - 2019 - academia.edu
... Korean missionaries and Cambodian church planters offer an ... Korean missionaries and Cambodian church planters has not ... Cambodia Bible College (CBC) church-planting projects in ...
☆ Save 🔊 Cite Related articles

11/15: Lunch with Park Hero

My college student in 1886 is now ready to go to Cambodia as a missionary for few years! I hooked him with a wonderful Cambodia missionary who's in USA to finish his PhD thesis! I loved to network with those whom I love and respect!

11/21: Riding trip in honor of Karl.

Robert Oh
12m · 🌐

Riding friends of Karl did a quick one-day riding trip to Malibu and Ojai town, California, yesterday. Appx 200 miles (320 km). We will miss riding with Karl!

Our riding buddy Karl passed away in September this year.

A few of us who loved him decided to do a day riding trip in honor of our friend. We started at Malibu beach Pier Café and rode to Ojai town up in the mountain and rode back home, passing through Magic Mountain. About 200 miles (320 km) trip. We will miss him!

11/23: Thanksgiving Family Dinner.

So thankful that we can celebrate Thanksgiving with our family!

11/28: Lunch with an old friend!

You know you are in good company when you don't have to worry about what you say and just be yourself. Here is a friend whom we ran the race together for such a long time we can just be ourselves! PTL!

249

My November Schedule page as an art form: This may become a collector's item 100 years later!

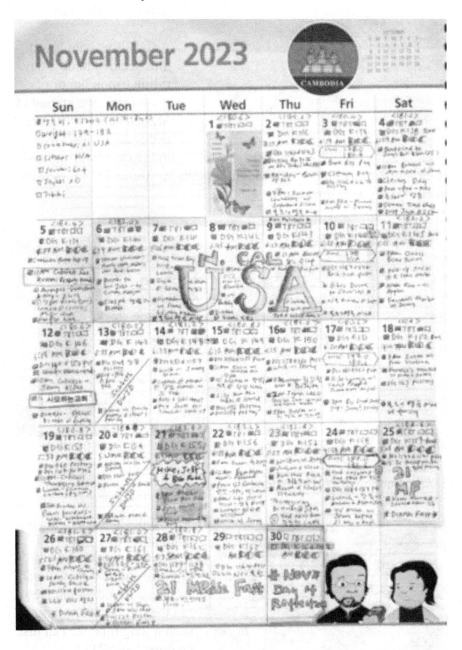

250

December

11/25-12/15: 21 days of media fast (& dinner fast).
Media fast is going great and helping me to focus on my writing –
PTL!

12/1: Living Like Kierkegaard: Nov. – was published today.

12/1: Commentary on Matthew, Part I was published today. Two
books in one day – Cool!

12/1: KAGMA meeting - consultation for the research project.
Started a consultation meeting by asking the question, "How
many Korean American missionaries are out there in the world?"
A very simple question but we weren't able to answer for last 36
years.

12/2: Took a family photo for our Christmas card.

12/2: Breakfast at IHOP

We take our Monday Sabbath seriously – especially ever since Jenny started her Doctor of Ministry course, learning about the importance of taking a day off from ministry. We had our brunch at International House of Pencake with Mom.

12/3: A gift from Korea – A full page report on our work in Cambodia. Translating Pastor Pang's book and teaching it at CPTI and other schools.

12/2: Catalyst - Big God small group party

Jenny and I really fell in love with these precious people of Catalyst Church of Long Beach. We feel their love and prayer even when we are traveling and engaging in mission work in Cambodia! PTL!

12/6: Attending Pastor Kim Jing Hong's Revival meeting

Pastor Jing Hong was my hero when I planted my first church in 1991. I was so sad that he couldn't remember me! We met in 1986 in Korea at Ture Village – my first mission trip to Korea. I wrote a book in honor of him many years ago.

Insight for the Day:
The word 'Traveling' comes from the Old French word *travil*, meaning "suffering or painful effort" or "trouble" as in traveling a long distance in a covered wagon. But remember, that was back before airplanes, G.P.S. units, and suitcases with wheels.

12/6: Brother Chris Song wrote an article about me – Cool!

캄보디아 리서치센터 대표·한국 키에르케고르 리서치센터 Oh TV '매일복음' 진행자 오석환 목사

바로 지금, 당신이 있는 그곳이 선교지입니다

목사님에 대한 전형적인 이미지가 있다면 청장차림에 한손에는 성경을 든 모습이다. 하지만 오석환 목사(영어명 Bob Oh)의 손에는 오토바이 헬멧이 함께 한다. 자신은 traffic jam(교통체증)이란 단어가 이해가 안된다고 너스레를 떠는 오 목사는 지난 2007년 캄보디아 선교를 위해 오토바이를 타고 미국 대륙을 일주하기도 했다. 30일간 총 8천 2백마일의 여정을 통해 펀드레이징 한 14만불로 캄보디아 선교를 시작한지도 23년차가 된다. 이 때 마련된 선교 후원금으로 캄보디아에 있는 목회자 자녀 35명을 4년제 대학을 보내기도 했다. 그때도 함께 했던 그의 애마 혼다 VTX 1300 오토바이는 20여년이 지난 지금도 그와 함께 하고 있다.

오 목사의 하루는 새벽 4시 반부터 시작된다. 말씀묵상과 기도로 시작하는 하루는 책을 집필하는데 유용한 시간이다. '느헤미아 리더쉽'(두레출판), '기도로 이끄는 삶'(Wipf & Stock), '힐링'(규장) 등의 베스트 셀러를 비롯, 지난 6월과 7월에는 'Real Self'(선교사로 사는 진정한 자신), '룻기서 주석'(Commentary Ruth)과 '키르케고르와 커피를 마시다'(Drinking Coffee with Kierkegaard), '키르케고르와 함께 살아가기'(Living Like Kierkegaard)가 아마존에서 출판되기도 했다. 현재까지 80여 권이 넘는 그의 출판물은 그의 목회자로서 그리고 선교사로의 삶의 고민과 그에 대한 해답이 고스란히 담겨져 있다.

빽빽한 스케줄이 담긴 그의 노트를 보면 복음증거자로서의 그의 삶이 얼마나 바쁜 지 짐작하게 한다. 지난 달에는 고등학교 12학년를 마치고 이제 막 대학교를 가는 아이들을 위한 JC Bridge Ministry 여름 수양회를 캘리포니아에서 인도하자 마자 덴마크 코펜하겐으로 이동, 키르케고르 리서치 센터를 방문했고 그 후 영국으로 건너가 집회 인도, 다시 캘리포니아에서 집회 인도 등 비록 이순의 나이를 넘겼지만 아직도 20대의 왕성한 체력과 영력으로 세계를 누비고 있다.

12/8: Prayer #10,147 – PPV! Public Prophetic Voice!

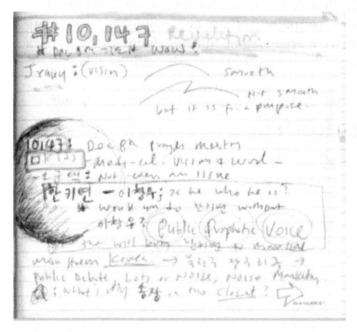

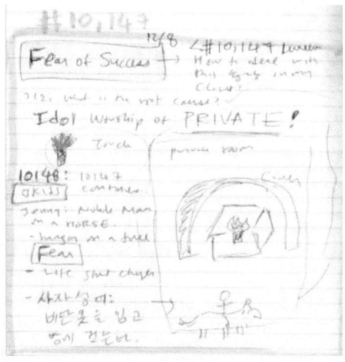

12/10: Brandon & Michelle Wedding.

Daniel and Esther's daughter Michelle got married today to Brandon. Never seen a whole wedding crew dancing before the meal. Very nice!

12/11: My first ChatGPT graphic! Authenicity
This graphic will change my life!

12/11: Time of meditation in my Cave!

12/11: The Sabbath date at Charley's Philly Steaks!

Robert Oh
2h

Enjoying a sabbath with my favorite wife! She loved Charley's cheesesteak sandwich! Thanks Charley!

12/12: I started teaching at America Evangelical University (AEU)

America Evangelical University

AEU's Mission statement: We offer an advanced theological educational program to meet the ever-increasing demand for qualified leadership in the fastest growing regions of the world. To that end, we integrate the Christian beliefs, character, and skills that will inspire our graduates to live out a holistic vision of the Kingdom of God.

Practically, we educate and train future Christian leaders, missionaries, and pastors based on sound Biblical principles and the best educational practices and methods. Our innovative partnership ensures high quality education within a contextually appropriate environment in which the Christian leaders are prepared to minister confidently and creatively within their culture.

12/16-22: Maui, Hawaii – Vacation with Jasos & Jane.

We are using our Time Share points at Westin Resort of Maui. So thankful that we learned how to do that after literally 10 years later – Thank you Stephen for figuring that out!

12/20-21: Kauai, Hawaii -Visiting my niece's daughter!

We gave up our 2 days stay at the resort to fly out to Kauai Island and meet Hazel – our new baby of the family! So was an angel and it was totally worth our sacrifice of time and money to be here! We even had privilege of watching Kainoa's first performance as a camel at the Nativity Story – PTL!

Kainoa as camel in the Nativity story! 5 Minutes. Dec. 2...

12/24: Family Christmas Eve dinner at San Diego - with Esther's family

We usually host a Christmas Eve party at our house. But since we were vacationing at Maui this year, we asked Jenny's sister Esther to host at her house. WOW! All the Oh family, Kang family and friends came with their dogs! I think we had more than 40 people at this party! Extrovert's heaven!

We are so thankful for His goodness in 2023!

It was so nice to receive a Christmas card from the Cambodia Oasis House staff today! God is so good! They had a wonderful Christmas party at Phnom Penh, Cambodia

12/29-30: The Well Church winter retreat.

 From their Web page: About Us - The Well Church is a new church plant that Sanctification Church is generously sharing its facilities with! That's the legal identity.

But who we are is a community of Christ followers who are helping one another become more and more mature disciples of Jesus Christ. In a word our goal is: DISCIPLESHIP.

Direction: We believe that our purpose is to become more and more like Jesus Christ. Or in other words to become HIS DISCIPLES. Why? This is what Jesus commanded His followers to do and we believe that this is what makes life worth living! Matt. 28:18 - 20. How? We believe that discipleship only happens in community. This happens when we are intentional in both formal and informal settings.

Our History: Many of our planting members have known each other for years and have gone through many life stages together. Through a variety of circumstances and challenges, God led this core group to plant a new church - something different then what they had been comfortable in. Our church was started in early 2022 meeting at homes and even for a while at a church in La Mirada. Then God began opening doors for us at our current location and we have been praying and clarifying our next steps in this journey. We love and appreciate our past church heritage, but we are looking forward to the challenge of making disciples of "all nations" through house church, community outreach and missions!

12/30: Berkeley Alumni dinner
12/31: Catalyst Church - Sunday service; Sermon

My December Schedule page as an art form: This may become a collector's item 100 years later!

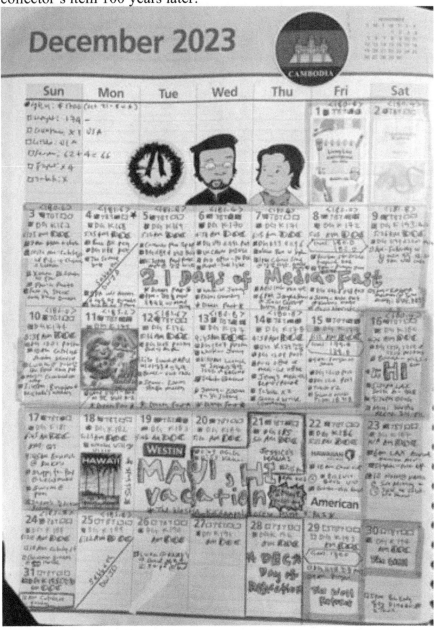

Appendix A: 2023 Publication

* I published 21books this year. That's total of 100 books in my life. PTL!

80. (1) Pillar of Fire & Cloud 2022, Kindle and Paperback by Amazon. (Jan)
81. (2) Commentary: Genesis, Part III. Kindle and Paperback by Amazon. (Jan)
82. (3) Commentary: Genesis, Part IV. Kindle and Paperback by Amazon. (Mar)
83. (4) 28 Days of Miracle. Kindle and Paperback by Amazon. (Mar)
84. (5) R.E.A.L. S.E.L.F.: To live as a Missionary in Los Angeles Post Covid. Kindle and Paperback by Amazon. (April)
85. (6) Commentary: Song of Songs. Kindle and Paperback by Amazon. (April)
86. (7) CPTI Church Planting Case Study Book. Kindle and Paperback by Amazon. (April)
87. (8) Commentary: Genesis, Part V. Kindle and Paperback by Amazon. (May)
88. (9) Commentary: Genesis – One Volume. Kindle and Paperback by Amazon. (May)
89. (10) Commentary: Ruth. Kindle and Paperback by Amazon. (July)
90. (11) Drinking Coffee with Kierkegaard: Kindle and Paperback by Amazon. (July)
91. (12) Living Like Kierkegaard: July, 2023. Kindle and Paperback by Amazon. (July)
92. (13) Commentary: Lamentations. Kindle and Paperback by Amazon. (August)
93. (14) Living Like Kierkegaard: August, 2023. Kindle and Paperback by Amazon. (August)
94. (15) Living Like Kierkegaard: September, 2023. Kindle and Paperback by Amazon. (September)

95. (16) Living Like Kierkegaard: October, 2023. Kindle and Paperback by Amazon. (October)
96. (17) Living Like Kierkegaard: November, 2023. Kindle and Paperback by Amazon. (November)
97. (18) Commentary: Matthew, Part I. Kindle and Paperback by Amazon. (Dec)
98. (19) Living Like Kierkegaard: December, 2023. Kindle and Paperback by Amazon. (December)
99. (20) Drinking Coffee with Kierkegaard: 2023. Kindle and Paperback by Amazon. (Dec)
100.   (21) Living Like Kierkegaard: 2023. Kindle and Paperback by Amazon. (Dec)

Appendix B: YouTube Posting in 2023

#MyYearOnYouTube2023

Dr Bob Oh TV

Member since 2019

Congratulations on a fantastic 2023 on YouTube! Here's a
look back on how you've grown as a creator. Share your
biggest highlights with all your fans on Shorts.

#MyYearOnYouTube2023

438
New subscribers

50.8K
Views

718
Uploads

2,261
Likes

12
Comments

533
Shares

Top video

72 hours watched

매일 복음 874일 & 밥 토크: 한국에서의 7일 간증. 2023년 2월 12일 (주일)

And that's a wrap on a great year!

Celebrate all your achievements this past year and
thank your fans on Shorts with
#MyYearOnYouTube2023.

We can't wait to see what you'll do in 2024.

Create a Short

These insights were taken from aggregated data from YouTube between
January 1, 2023, and November 30, 2023.

Appendix C: Academia.Edu posting in 2023

245 million scholars subscribe to this Web site, and around 140,000 people join Academia.edu each day. I have been posting video, papers, and books here since 2009 at Oxford, UK.

In 2023, I have followers and ranked top 3% contributor! PTL!

Robert Oh

Oxford Centre For Mission Studies, Missiology, Post-Doc

Academia Response on downloading.

- V. V. from Cambodia left a reason for downloading A Reflection on the Influence of the Church Growth Movement in Cambodia (2028 words). Dear professor, I have downloaded. This will help me in my pastor cell group. Thanks for sharing. God bless you!

- M. H. from USA left a reason for downloading Cambodia Research & Resource Center: Research Publication 2020 - Ministry to Khmer in the USA.

- K. J. from Korea left a reason for downloading Dr. Bob Oh's Poetry on Chun Sang Byung and Søren Kierkegaard. Dear,Thanks to your kindness, I got the paper on Poet Bob Oh!

- L. H. W. from Korea left a reason for downloading Commentary: Lamentations. I can read the commentary on Lamentations while listening to his Daily Gospel.

- S. M. from America (A Micro and Small Business Entrepreneurship) left a reason for downloading Dr. Bob Oh's 21 Days of Fasting and Prayer. A sermon you gave at our church

- J. M. an Independent Researcher & Student, left a reason for downloading The Christian Life. You did Great work sir. thank you.

- Y. B. M. from Cambodia left a reason for downloading on Patron Client paper. Thank you for this paper.

- N. S. left a reason for downloading Dr Bob Oh's Lecture: Tithing (English and Korean Edition) - Thank you so much for your book on Tithing.

- J. P. of Korea wrote: Are there more videos of your Christian Framework series? I hope to see more! Thank you for sharing! I'm so blessed by you and Jenny!

- K. O. of Nigeria left a reason for downloading Dr. Bob Oh's Lecture: PhD Research Induction School Notes - Dear Robert, I listened to your presentation of your story after your PhD award at the OCMS chapel. The mobilization of funds and partnership across the USA with power Bike was amazing and terrific. Looking forward to contacting you by email. How are the school and ministries in Cambodia?

Point: I had scholars from Saudi Arabia reading my book in Korean! Awesome!

← **ACADEMIA**

Recent Activity   183 Visits

Prayer Driven Life in Chinese Edition
The Netherlands · Rotterdam
Sunday, December 17, 2023 · google.nl

기도로 이끄는 삶
Saudi Arabia · Riyadh
Saturday, December 16, 2023 · google.com

Commentary on I Corinthians, Part 1
Vietnam · Ho Chi Minh City
Saturday, December 16, 2023 · academia.edu

Appendix D: GBS Radio posting in 2023

Since November 2020, I aired weekly 'Book Talk' through Global Broadcasting System Internet Radio reaching 7.5 million diaspora Koreans all over the world. PTL!

Support Information

I greet you in the Lord Jesus Christ.

Thank you so much for your love and support for our work in Cambodia!

Robert Oh

◆Email: oikosbishop@mac.com

◆ Internet:
www.blesscambodia.com
* You can use PayPal from this site.

◆ USA :
KAGMA (Korean American Global Mission Association)
*Write the check to: KAGMA and Note: 'Cambodia Project'
PO Box 4885
Cerritos, CA 90703

◆ Korea :
KEB Hana Bank
Acct : 166-18-07737-7
Name : Oh Sukhwan

Made in the USA
Monee, IL
10 January 2024

50553243R00154